Liberal Party of Canada

# Platform of the Liberal Party of Canada

Liberal Party of Canada

**Platform of the Liberal Party of Canada**

ISBN/EAN: 9783744662116

Printed in Europe, USA, Canada, Australia, Japan

Cover: Foto ©Suzi / pixelio.de

More available books at **www.hansebooks.com**

# ATFORM

OF

# THE LIBERAL PARTY

OF

# CANADA.

---

Exemplified by Quotations, Tables and Arguments

Based on Census and Trade Returns.

---

CHARLOTTETOWN, P. E. ISLAND:

GEO. W. GARDINER, STEAM PRINTER, QUEEN STREET.

1895.

# LIBERAL PLATFORM

## —ADOPTED BY THE—

# National Liberal Convention,

## OTTAWA,

## JUNE, 1893.

---

We, the Liberal Party of Canada, in convention assembled declare

### 1.—FREER TRADE—REDUCED TAXATION.

That the customs tariff of the Dominion should be based, not as it is now, upon the protective principle, but upon the requirements of the public service ;

That the existing tariff, founded upon an unsound principle, and used, as it has been by the Government, as a corrupting agency wherewith to keep themselves in office has developed monopolies, trusts and combinations ;

It has decreased the value of farm and other landed property .

It has oppressed the masses to the enrichment of a few;

It has checked immigration ;

It has caused great loss of population ;

It has impeded commerce|;

It has discriminated against Great Britain ;

In these and in many other ways it has occasioned great public and private injury, all of which evils must continue to grow in intensity as long as the present tariff system r͡    ͞ ͞ns in force.

That the highest interests of Canada demand a removal of this obstacle to our country's progress by the adoption of a sound fiscal policy. which, while not doing injustice to any class, will promote domestic and foreign trade, and hasten the return of prosperity to our people.

That to that end, the tariff should be reduced to the needs of honest, economical and efficient government;

That it should be so adjusted as to make free, or to bear as lightly as possible upon, the necessaries of life, and should be so arranged as to promote freer trade with the whole world, more particularly with Great Britain and the United States.

We believe that the results of the protective system have grievously disappointed thousands of persons who honestly supported it, and that the country, in the light of experience, is now prepared to declare for a sound fiscal policy.

The issue between the two political parties on this question is now clearly defined.

The Government themselves admit the failure of their fiscal policy and now profess their willingness to make some changes; but they say that such changes must be based only on the principle of protection.

We denounce the principle of protection as radically unsound and unjust to the masses of the people, and we declare our conviction that any tariff changes based on that principle must fail to afford any substantial relief from the burdens under which the country labors.

This issue we unhesitatingly accept, and upon it we await with the fullest confidence the verdict of the electors of Canada.

## 2.—ENLARGED MARKETS—RECIPROCITY.

That having regard to the prosperity of Canada and the United States as adjoining countries, with many mutual interests, it is desirable that there should be the most friendly relations, and broad and liberal trade intercourse between them ;

That the interests alike of the Dominion and of the Empire would be materially advanced by the establishing of such relations;

That the period of the old reciprocity treaty was one of marked prosperity to the British North American colonies ;

That the pretext under which the Government appealed to the country in 1891 respecting negotiation for a treaty with the United States was misleading and dishonest, and intended to deceive the electorate;

That no sincere effort has been made by them to obtain a treaty, but that, on the contrary, it is manifest that the present Government, controlled as they are by monopolies and combines, are not desirous of securing such a treaty ;

That the first step towards obtaining the end in view, is to place a party in power who are sincerely desirous of promoting a treaty on terms honorable to both countries ;

That a fair and liberal reciprocity treaty would develop the great natural resources of Canada, would enormously increase the trade and commerce between the two countries, would tend to encourage friendly relations between the two peoples, would remove many causes which have in the past provoked irritation and trouble to the Governments of both countries, and would promote those kindly relations between the Empire and the Republic which afford the best guarantee for peace and prosperity.

That the Liberal party is prepared to enter into negotiations with a view to obtaining such a treaty, including a well considered list of manufactured articles, and we are satisfied that any treaty so arranged will receive the assent of Her Majesty's Government, without whose approval no treaty can be made.

## 3.—PURITY OF ADMINISTRATION—CONDEMN CORRUPTION.

That the Convention deplores the gross corruption in the management and expenditure of public moneys which for years past has existed under the rule of the Conservative party, and the revelations of which by the different parliamentary committees of inquiry have brought disgrace upon the fair name of Canada.

The Government which profited politically by these expenditures of public moneys of which the people have been defrauded, and which, nevertheless, have never punished the guilty parties, must be held responsible for the wrongdoing. We arraign the Government for retaining in office a Minister of the Crown proved to have accepted very large contributions of money for election purposes from the funds of a railway company, which, while paying the political contributions to him, a member of the Government with one hand, was receiving Government subsidies with the other.

The conduct of the Minister and the approval of his colleagues, after the proof became known to them, are calculated to degrade Canada in the estimation of the world, and deserve the severe condemnation of the people.

## 4.-DEMAND STRICTEST ECONOMY.-DECREASED EXPENDITURE.

We cannot but view with alarm the large increase of the public debt and of the controllable annual expenditure of the Dominion and the consequent undue taxation of the people under the Governments that have been continuously in power since 1878, and we demand the strictest economy in the administration of the government of the country.

## 5—FOR RESPONSIBLE GOVERNMENT—INDEPENDENCE OF PARLIAMENT.

That the Convention regrets that by the action of Ministers and their supporters in Parliament, in one case in which serious charges were made against a Minister of the Crown, investigation was altogether refused, while in another case the charges preferred were altered and then referred to a commission appointed upon the advice of the Ministry, contrary to the well settled practice of Parliament; and this Convention affirm:

That it is the ancient and undoubted right of the House of Commons to inquire into all matters of public expenditure, and into all charges of misconduct in office against Ministers of the Crown, and the reference of such matters to royal commission created upon the advice of the accused is at variance with the due responsibility of Ministers to the House of Commons, and tends to weaken the authority of the House over the Executive Government, and this convention affirms that the powers of the people's representatives in this regard should on all fitting occasions be upheld.

## 6—THE LAND FOR THE SETTLER—NOT FOR THE SPECULATOR.

That in the opinion of this Convention the sales of public lands of the Dominion should be to actual settlers only, and not to speculators, upon reasonable terms of settlement, and in such areas as can be reasonably occupied and cultivated by the settler.

## 7.—OPPOSE THE DOMINION FRANCHISE ACT—FAVOR THE PROVINCIAL FRANCHISE.

That the Franchise Act since its introduction has cost the Dominion Treasury over a million dollars, besides entailing a heavy expenditure to both political parties.

That each revision involves an additional expenditure of a further quarter of a million;

That this expenditure has prevented an annual revision, as originally intended, in the absence of which young voters entitled to the franchise have, in numerous instances, been prevented from exercising their natural rights.

That it has failed to secure uniformity, which was the principal reason assigned for its introduction;

That it has produced gross abuses by partizan revising barristers appointed by the Government of the day;

That its provisions are less liberal than those already existing in many Provinces of the Dominion, and that in the opinion of this Convention the Act should be repealed, and we should revert to the Provincial Franchise.

## 8.—AGAINST THE GERRYMANDER—COUNTY BOUNDARIES SHOULD BE PRESERVED

That by the Gerrymander Acts, the electoral divisions for the return of members to the House of Commons have been so made as to prevent a fair expression of the opinion of the country at the general elections, and to secure to the party now in power a strength out of all proportion greater than the number of electors supporting them would warrant. To put an end to this abuse, to make the House of Commons a fair exponent of public opinion, and to preserve the historic continuity of counties, it is desirable that in the formation of electoral divisions, county boundaries be preserved, and that in no case parts of different counties should be put in one electoral division.

## 9—THE SENATE DEFECTIVE—AMEND THE CONSTITUTION.

The present constitution of the Senate is inconsistent with the Federal principal in our system of government, and is in other respects defective, as it makes the Senate independent of the people and uncontrolled by the public opinion of the country, and should be so amended as to bring it into harmony with the principles of popular government.

## 10—QUESTION OF PROHIBITION—A DOMINION PLEBISCITE.

That whereas public attention is at present much directed to the consideration of the admittedly great evils of intemperance, it is desirable that the mind of the people should be clearly ascertained on the question of Prohibition by means of a Dominion Plebiscite.

# A PRIMER OF TARIFF REFORM.

Q. What is a tariff?

A. A tariff is a tax imposed on commodities imported from foreign countries.

Q. What is a tax?

A. A tax is the portion of property or product which the Government takes (by compulsion) from every citizen—not a pauper—for public purposes.

Q. What are public purposes, in the sense of this definition?

A. A definition given by the Supreme Court was as follows: "For the purpose of carrying on the Government in all its machinery and operations."

Q. What is free trade?*

A. Free trade is the right of every man to freely exchange the products of his labor and services in such a way as seems to him most advantageous, subject only to such restrictions as the State may find necessary to make for the purposes of revenue or for sanitary or moral considerations. Conversely, it is the denial of the right of a free government to arbitrarily take from any person any portion of the product of his labor for the benefit of some other man who has not earned or paid for it.

---

* The following definitions of free trade and protection appeared in the Philadelphia *American*, of August 7th, 1884. a representative protectionist paper:

"The term Free Trade, although much discussed, is seldom rightly defined. It does not mean the abolition of custom houses. Nor does it mean the substitution of direct for indirect taxation, as a few American disciples of the school have supposed. It means such an adjustment of taxes on imports as will cause no diversion of capital from any channel into which it would otherwise flow, into any channel opened or favored by the legislation which enacts the customs. A country may collect its entire revenue by duties on imports, and yet be an entirely Free Trade country, *so long as it does not lay those duties in such a way as to lead anyone to undertake any employment or make any investment he would avoid in the absence of such duties.* Thus, the customs duties levied by England—with a very few exceptions—are not inconsistent with her profession of being a country that believes in Free Trade. They either are duties on articles not produced in England, or they are exactly equivalent to the excise duties levied on the same articles if made at home. They do not lead anyone to put his money into the home production of an article, because they do not discriminate in favor of the home producer. It is therefore no concession to the protective principle when the Democratic platform says that 'since the foundation of the government custom house duties have furnished its main source of revenue,' and that 'this system must continue.'

"A protective duty, on the other hand, has for its object to effect the diversion of a part of the capital and labor of the people out of the channels in which it would run otherwise, into channels favored or created by law."

Q. What is protection?

A. Protection, on the ground of advantages accruing directly or incidentally, advocates and defends the imposition of taxes on imports for other purposes than those of revenue. The protective system is opposed to the revenue system because the Government collects revenue on what comes in, while protection is secured only to the extent to which commodities are kept out.

Q. What is the idea underlying each?

A. Free trade assumes that a people like those of Canada might be left to themselves to decide what is to their own advantage; Protection assumes that Parliament can better decide what business the people shall do than the people themselves.

Q. What is a tariff for revenue only?

A. A "tariff for revenue only" is one so framed that all the taxes which the people pay, the Government shall receive.

Q. What is meant by a tariff for revenue with "incidental protection?"

A. The adjustment of a tariff for revenue in such a way as to afford what is termed "incidental protection" is based on the supposition that by arranging a scale of duties so moderate as only to restrict and not prevent importations, it is possible to secure sufficient revenue for the State, and at the same time stimulate domestic manufactures by increasing the price of competitive foreign products.

Q. Is this double object capable of attainment?

A. Undoubtedly; but it is also one of the most costly of all methods of raising revenue. For while revenue to the State accrues only from the tax levied on what is imported, another tax, arising from an increase of price, is also paid by the nation upon all domestic products that are sold and consumed in competition with the foreign article. A tariff for revenue so adjusted as to afford incidental protection, is therefore a system which requires the consumers, who are the people, to pay much in order that the State may receive little.

## PROTECTION INVOLVES THE PRINCIPLE OF SLAVERY.

Q. What is the highest right of property?

A. The right to freely exchange it for other property.

Q. How do you prove this?

A. If all exchange of property were forbidden, each individual would be like Robinson Crusoe on his uninhabited island. He would have to live on what he individually produced or collected, and would be deprived of all benefits of co-operation with his fellow-men, and of all the advantages of production that come from diversity of skill or diversity of natural circumstances. In the absence of all freedom of exchange between man and man, civilization would be impossible; and to the degree in which we impede or obstruct the freedom of exchange--i. e., commercial intercourse,--to that same degree we oppose the development of civilization.

Q. Is it the intent and result of a "protective" tariff to restrict exchanges?

A. It invariably amounts to the same thing, whether we make the interchange of commodities costly and difficult by interposing deserts, swamps, unbridged streams, bad roads or bands of robbers between producers and consumers, or whether, for the benefit of some private interests, that have done nothing to merit it, we impose a toll on the commodities transported, and call it a tariff. In both cases there is a greater effort and an increased cost required to produce a given result, and a diminution of the abundance of the things which minister to everybody's necessities, comfort and happiness. A twenty per cent duty is like a bad road; a fifty per cent., like a broad, deep and rapid river, without any proper facilities for crossing, a seventy-five per cent., like a swamp flanking such a river on both sides; while a hundred per cent. duty, such as is levied upon kerosene oil, is as a band of robbers, who strip the merchant of nearly all he possesses, and make him not a little grateful that he escapes with his life.

Q. How does a tariff, enacted for so-called "protection," involve the principle of slavery?

A. Any system of law which denies to an individual the right freely to exchange the products of his labor, by declaring that A, a citizen, may trade on equal terms with B, another citizen, but shall not under equally favorable circumstances trade with C, who lives in another country, reaffirms in effect the principle of slavery. For both slavery and the artificial restriction of exchanges deny to the individual the right to use the products of his labor according to his own pleasure, or what may seem to him the best advantage. In other words, the practical working of both the system of human slavery and the system of protection is to deprive the individual of a portion of the fruits of his labor, without making in return any direct compensation.

Q. What is the argument generally put forth by protectionists to justify the restriction of freedom of exchanges?

A. That any PRESENT loss or injury resulting from such restriction to the individual will be more than compensated to him INDIRECTLY, as a citizen of the State.

Q. Was not this essentially the argument used to justify slavery?

A. Yes. The plea for slavery asserted that the system was really for the good of the slaves, and that any deprivation endured by them for the good of society—meaning the masters—would be fully compensated to them, through moral discipline, if not in this world, certainly in the world to come. It made the slave-owners, who enacted the laws, the sole judges of the question.

Q. Have not the same arguments employed for the restriction of exchanges—i. e., indirect or future individual or social benefit as a justification for present personal restriction or injury—been always used to justify every encroachment by despotic governments on the freedom of the individual?

A. Yes; and especially in warrant of State persecution for heresy or unbelief; of enforced conformity with State religions; of abridging the liberty of speech and of the press and of restricting the right of suffrage. In short, the restriction of freedom of exchange for the purpose of subserving private interests, is one of those acts on the part of the State which are utterly antagonistic to the the principles of free government; and which, if fully carried out, would be absolutely destructive of it.

# 'THE TWO POLICIES.

What are the broad distinctions dividing the two great political parties in Canada?

FREE TRADE as against PROTECTION, RECIPROCITY as against RESTRICTION, and *Honest Economical Government* as against the *Extravagance, Mismanagement* and *Corruption* which has characterized Canada's Government for years past!

Other important issues relating to *The Senate, Prohibition* and other matters also divide the parties, but at present the great *Trade Question* over-rides all else.

The policy known as the N. P., which has been in force since 1878, is sought to be still longer retained by the Conservatives.

Its basic principle is the imposition of duties so high that foreign manufactures will be excluded, and their manufacture in Canada encouraged and promoted, and the argument used is that domestic competition will be sufficient to keep prices down and prevent the consumer being fleeced.

The Liberals object to this policy as being unjust to the State, unjust to the consumer, and calculated to promote extravagance and to diminish instead of enlarge our commerce

They contend that the experience of the sixteen years past has confirmed their predictions, and that in the words of the Ottawa platform the N. P. has

1. Decreased the value of farm and other landed property.
2. Oppressed the masses to the enrichment of a few.
3. Checked immigration.
4. Caused great loss of population.
5. Impeded commerce.
6. Discriminated against Great Britain.

The taxes collected under the N. P. and paid direct to the Treasury have since the year 1878 amounted to nearly ONE HUNDRED MILLIONS OF DOLLARS more than would have been taken out of the people had the McKenzie revenue tariff been maintained instead of the N. P. tariff.

Notwithstanding this enormous increase of taxation there was a

## DEFICIT

last year of $1,000,000 odd, and this year it is very much greater. The DEFICIT, as the returns up to end of January, 1895, show, will reach at the end of the fiscal year, Five Millions of Dollars.

But the *excessive taxation* laid upon the people and *paid into the Treasury* is only a small proportion of the *real taxation*, the greater part of which the people *are compelled to pay to the protected industries.*

The ·best authories place this at \$2 for every \$1 paid to the Treasury.

Even if it were only equal to that paid into- the Treasury it would be enormous.

The question arises right on the threshold of the argument, why should a law be passed enabling one man or several men formed into a company, to compel people to pay him or them a much larger sum for the goods they bny than they would be obliged to pay in the open market.

If any particular man, say John Smith, was able to get a law passed at Ottawa saying that he should have a monopoly in Canada of the sale of any particular article, whether rope, cotton, iron, woolens, oil, rice, sugar or any other article, and should have the right to charge what price he pleased up to a certain fixed price far beyond that for which it could be purchased abroad, every elector would at onee say: Why, that's an immoral and unjust and an unfair law.

And yet the N. P. tariff is just such a law and has just such an effect, the only difference being that its favorites are as a rule COMPANIES and not individuals.

## THE N. P. MONOPOLY.

Experience has shown that when *foreign goods* are excluded and the Canadian market kept close for Canadian manufactures, unrestrained by foreign competition, the result is the formation of COMBINES AND MONOPOLIES, which control the market, buy up all Canadian competition and charge the consumer for his goods *the utmost limit the law (N. P.) allows.*

Such to-day is the case with CORDAGE, COTTONS, WOOLENS, SUGAR, ETC., ETC., ETC.

For a few years internal competition had the effect of keeping down the prices, but as the Canadian market was a limited one, the factories soon cut each other's throats, and now either by a MONOPOLY, such as exists in the cotton and cordage trade, or by a monopoly as in the iron trade, competition does not exist, the ordinary laws regulating prices are ignored, and these pet industries are enable to fleece the consumer at their own sweet will, and all by virtue of a law passed by the people fleeced.

## THE LIBERAL POLICY.

The policy of the Liberal party is in the first place:

1. To reduce the annual expenditure to the lowest sum compatible with honest economical government.

2. To abolish all unnecessary expenditures and curtail and reduce those which, though necessary, are extravagant.

3. To raise by taxation only just so much money as is absolutely necessary to carry on the government.

4. To so adjust the customs tariff that ALL THE TAXES PAID THROUGH IT SHALL GO INTO THE TREASURY AND NOT INTO THE COFFERS OF A FEW FAVORED INDUSTRIES.

The present Government say they cannot "run the machinery" for less than the present expenditure, and that the present customs tariff (which collects $20,000,000 for the Treasury and more than $20,000,000 besides for the combines, trusts and other protected industries) is the best they can devise.

Mr. Foster, in his Budget speech of 1894, expressly and deliberately stated THAT THE MAIN OBJECT IN FRAMING A TARIFF OUGHT NOT TO BE TO RAISE REVENUE FOR THE COUNTRY, BUT TO DEVELOP THE INDUSTRIES OF THE COUNTRY.

His exact words were : " So far as the revenue aspect is " concerned, it is OF INFINITELY LESS IMPORTANCE than " the effect and details of the tariff upon the trade and develop " ment of a country."

As opposed to all this

The Liberal party says that several millions may be lopped off the present expenditure without injuring the public service. (Hon. D. Mills estimates the possible saving at $4,000,000.)

The Liberals further say that while all citizens according to their means should be taxed for the support of the national government, to tax them for the support of private enterprises, and under cover of law to take money from one citizen's purse to enrich another, is a gross injustice and "legalized robbery."

Now in order properly to understand the working of the N. P. we ought to consider carefully how we *stood financially in 1878*, how we stand financially to-day, and how our present DEBT, TAXATION AND EXPENDITURE compares with that of the revenue tariff period of Mr. McKenzie, and how that great test of national wealth and progress, viz.: the population of the country stands and compares with former periods.

At the end of the financial year 1878, when Mr. McKenzie went out of power, the nett debt of the Dominion was $140,362,069.91.

# DEBT AND EXPENDITURE LARGELY INCREASED.

The Conservative Government has increased this debt since then nearly $110,000,000, until, as shown by the Canada Gazette of February 7, it stood, 31 January, 1895, at close upon $250,000,000. equal to $50 for every man, woman and child in the Dominion.

Now it may well be asked by any man in the Maritime Provinces How much of this $110,000,000 increased public debt has been spent in the Maritime Provinces? Of course a large sum went to pay for the Canadian Pacific Railway and other large sums in building new canals and deepening others, but after making every reasonable allowance for important and necessary PUBLIC WORKS, it is evident that there must have been GROSS AND UNBOUNDED EXTRAVAGANCE, while in many cases the country was DEFRAUDED AND ROBBED.

Taking each ten years and starting at Confederation we find the nett debt as follows:   (See Public Accounts, 1894, p. xxx.)

| | |
|---|---|
| 1867 | $ 75,728,641.37 |
| 1877 | 132,235,309.00 |
| 1887 | 227,314,775.44 |
| 1894 | 246,183,029.48 |
| 1895, Jan. 31 | 249,407,462.55 |

Now look at our nett taxes paid to the Government during same periods.  These taxes consist of customs and excise duties alone.

| | | |
|---|---|---|
| In 1867 we paid in taxes, | - | $ 11,700,681.08 |
| " 1877 " " | - | 17,697,924.00 |
| " 1887 " " | - | 28,687,000.00 |
| " 1894 " " | - | 27,579,203.00 |

(See Public Accounts, 1894, p. xxxii.)

In the intervening years of 1889, 1890 and 1891 we paid respectively $30,613,522, $31,587,071, and $30,314,151.

Now while the public debt and the taxes have increased as shown, how has the annual expenditure been maintained?

We give the figures taken from the Public Accounts as follows:

## TOTAL EXPENDITURE.

| | |
|---|---|
| 1867-8 | $ 13,486,092.00 |
| 1877-8 | 23,503,158.25 |
| 1887-8 | 36,718,494.79 |
| 1893-4 | 37,585,025.52 |

# INCREASED THE TAXES.

It will thus be seen that while the Conservatives have INCREASED the people's taxes ACTUALLY PAID INTO THE TREASURY by over $10,000,000 each year since they came into power in 1878, they have also increased the annual expenditure over that incurred in Mr. McKenzie's time over $14,000,000 yearly, and at the same time have added to the public nett debt $110,000,000. The following figures show the comparison between 1878 and 1894.

|  | 1878. | 1894. |
|---|---|---|
| Customs taxation, - | $ 12,782,824 | $ 19,198,114 |
| Total taxation, - | 17,841,938 | 27,579,203 |
| Expenditure, - - | 23,503,158 | 37,585,025 |
| Nett debt, - - - | 140,362,069 | 249,407,462 |

These enormous sums can hardly be fully appreciated by an average man. But comparisons with other countries may assist in enabling one to grasp their meaning.

Great Britain has for more than a century past been engaged in costly wars by land and sea and in all parts of the world. She has had necessarily to pile up an enormous public debt. Yet to-day the annual charge for the PUBLIC DEBT OF GREAT BRITAIN is only 31 per cent. of its revenue, while that of Canada is not less than 41 per cent. In other words. Great Britain has, out of every $100 of revenue collected by customs and excise taxes, to put by $31 to defray the annual charges of it public debt; while out of every $100 Canada collects by customs and excise taxes she has to put by $41 to defray the annual charges of her debt. These charges embrace the interest on the debt and the sinking fund which we are obliged by law to keep up.

Now look at the UNITED STATES. Their debt practically speaking is paid off. It is now only $12 per head of the population and it only takes $7 out of every $100 they collect by customs and excise taxes to pay the interest and charges upon it.

So that while CANADA has to take $41 out of every $100 she collects by customs and excise taxes to pay the interest and charges on her debt, GREAT BRITAIN only has to take $31 for a similar purpose, and the UNITED STATES only $7.

But the Tory orator says under the McKenzie Government you had nothing but

# DEFICITS,

while the Conservative Government has had a series of surplusses. This statement is far from accurate. The Public Accounts shows, p. xxxiii., that there were surpluses in 1873-74 of $888,775.79—1874-75 of $935,644.00.

It is true that in the three following years there were deficits as follows : 1875-76—$1,900,785—1876-77 1,460,027—1877-78—1,128,146.

But it must never be forgotten that these deficits were not incurred by any extravagance or increase in the expenditure but because the taxation of the people was reduced. As a matter of fact nearly $3,000,000 less taxes were raised in each of the years 1876-77 and 1877-78 than were raised in 1873-74 or 1874-75 and of course many millions less than the Tory Government has since raised.

The reduction was mainly caused by the cheapness of goods imported, the customs duties being levied by an ad valorem rate or so much per hundred upon the cost. It is manifest therefor that if and when the cost of the goods imported is reduced say one-third, the tax paid by the people to the Government is greatly reduced, so it was in the three years referred to owing to the world wide depression then existing and thus it was that deficits occurred.

Governments are as a rule only blameable for deficits when they are guilty of EXTRAVAGANT OR INJUSTIFIABLE EXPENDITURE and not simply because the amount of taxation they raise from the people is small.

But what is the record of the Tory Government since 1878 in this point.

## DEFICITS.

| | | | | | |
|---|---|---|---|---|---|
| In 1878-9 the deficit was | - | - | $1,937,999 |
| " 1879-80 " " | - | - | 1,543,227 |
| " 1884-5 " " | - | - | 2,240,058 |
| " 1885-6 " " | - | - | 5,834,571 |
| " 1887-8 " " | - | - | 810,031 |
| " 1893-4 " " | - | - | 1,210,332 |

For the present year 1895 the returns are of course not complete but we have the official returns for the seven months ending January 31st, published in Canada Gazette and they show that while there was a deficit of $1,210,332 for the whole year

1893-4 the REVENUE for the seven months ending January 1895 was $2,159,720 less than for the corresponding period in 1893-4 while the expenditure was $738,310 greater. We are therefore almost THREE MILLION DOLLARS worse off on the 31st January 1895, than on 31st January 1894, and THE DEFICIT when the fiscal year ends on 1st July, CANNOT WELL BE LESS THAN FIVE MILLIONS and may considerably exceed it.

With our financial condition thus DARK, with huge deficits and a rapidly falling revenue, with our taxes increased to the limit of the people's endurnce, the Government, instead of curtailing expenditure, have largely increased it; while our debt has reached figures which almost force thoughtful men to doubt our future.

## GREAT LOSS OF POPULATION.

The CENSUS RETURNS show that excluding altogether the 886,000 immigrants who camej to Canada during the ten years, 1881 to 1891, there should have been an increase of population by NATURAL INCREASE ALONE (calculated at 2 p.c. a year) of not less than 900,000. The actual increase was in round figures 500,000. The LOSS IN NATIVE BORN POPULATION WAS THEREFORE IN THE TEN YEARS 400,000. If to this however be added the 886,000 immigrants who according to the statistics of the department of agriculture were brought into this country during these ten years at a cost of according to the Public Accounts, p. iiv. about $3,000,000, the actual exodus from Canada during the ten years 1881 to 1891 amounted to OVER 1,200,000 PERSONS or 120,000 EACH YEAR. The United States census agrees with ours in this regard and shows that of every male born in Canada, between the ages of twenty and fifty years, one in three is found in the United States.

The following Table is compiled from the census returns by the Dominion Statistician Johnson and published in the Statistical Year Book for 1893, p. 119.

### POPULATION OF CANADA, 1871, 1881 AND 1891.

| PROVINCES. | 1871 | 1881 | Increase, Per Cent. | 1891 | Increase, Per Cent. |
|---|---|---|---|---|---|
| Ontario, | 1,620,851 | 1,926,922 | 18.6 | 2,114,321 | 9.73 |
| Quebec, | 1,191,516 | 1,359,027 | 14.0 | 1,488,535 | 9.53 |
| Nova Scotia, | 387,800 | 440,572 | 13.6 | 450,396 | 2.23 |
| New Brunswick, | 285,594 | 321,233 | 12.4 | 321,263 | NONE |
| Manitoba, | 18,995 | 62,260 | 247.2 | 152,506 | 144.95 |
| British Columbia, | 36,247 | 40,459 | 36.4 | 98,173 | 98.49 |
| Prince Ed. Island, | 94,021 | 108,891 | 15.8 | 109,078 | 0.17 |
| The Territories, | | 56,446 | | 98,967 | 75.33 |

These official figures show that the Maritime Provinces have suffered in the matter of the exodus worse than any of the others, having lost during the ten years between 1881 and 1891 allowing for natural increase of the population 165,000 PERSONS.

The increase of population in the Maritime Provinces between 1871 and 1881 was 103,281 allowing for natural increase at 2 per cent. a year it should have been 153,480.

The Exodus therefore during that period reached 50,000 or 5000 a year.

The increase between 1881 and 1891 was only 10,000. Allowing for natural increase at 2 per cent. a year, it should have been 175,000.

The exodus therefore during that period was 165,000 or 16,500 each year.

During the revenue tariff period, therefore, which covered nearly all the years 1871 to 1881 the prosperity of the Maritime Provinces, as evidenced by increase of population, if not all that could be desired, was at least respectable.

During the ten years of a protective policy that prosperity, as similarly evidenced, was altogether wanting. An exodus of 165,000 persons in ten years from a population of 870,696, inhabiting such a rich and highly favored part of the world as Nova Scotia, New Brunswick and P. E. Island, is APPALLING.

But, say the Protectionists, people have gone to Manitoba and the Northwest and British Columbia.

Would that it were so. The inexorable facts recorded in the census returns absolutely disprove any such theory. They show that the total number of Maritime Province people to be found in 1891 in Manitoba, Northwest Territories and British Columbia was 4,280. What became of the other 160,000? Every one knows THEY WENT TO THE UNITED STATES.

## NEW BRUNSWICK UNDER THE N. P.

That the Province of New Brunswick has not prospered under the N. P. is very apparent. A simple statement of facts speaks eloquently against a protective tariff. Despite its vast forest wealth, agricultural resources and valuable fisheries, it presents arrested development. Note this contrast :—

Increased population from 1871 to 1881　-　-　-　35,639
Increased population from 1881 to 1891 only　-　-　-　30

The city of Moncton, through its favorable situation as a railway centre has, through special causes, grown rapidly in both decades; and deducting the increase in the city of Moncton the statistics for the entire province outside the city is rather startling. Note the contrast :—

Provincial Increase (less Moncton) from 1871 to 1881　- 32,207
Provincial DECREASE (less Moncton) from 1881 to 1891　3,703

This is the province, one of whose representatives, Sir Leonard Tilley, as finance minister advised the merchants to clap on full sail for twenty years of prosperity.

But again the Protectionist argues the tendency has been of late years for the rural population to migrate to the cities.

Has that been the case in the Maritime Provinces? Unfortunately, no! The people have left us altogether.

Look at the following tables compiled from the census reports and to be found on pages 123 and 124 of the Government Statistical Abstract for 1894:

# POPULATION OF CANADA BY ELECTORAL DISTRICTS, 1891 and 1881.
## Nova Scotia.

| Electoral Districts. | 1881. | 1891. | Increase or Decrease Number. | Per Cent. |
|---|---|---|---|---|
| Annapolis | 20,598 | 19,350 | —1,248 | — 6·0 |
| Antigonish | 18,060 | 16,114 | —1,946 | —10·7 |
| Cape Breton | 31,258 | 34,244 | 2,986 | 9·6 |
| Colchester | 26,720 | 27,160 | 440 | 1·6 |
| Cumberland | 27,368 | 34,529 | 7,161 | 26·1 |
| Digby | 19,881 | 19,897 | 16 | |
| Guysborough | 17,808 | 17,195 | — 613 | — 3·4 |
| Halifax (City) | 36,100 | 38,495 | 2,395 | 6·8 |
| Halifax (County) | 31,817 | 32,863 | 1,046 | 3·3 |
| Hants | 23,359 | 22,052 | —1,307 | — 5·6 |
| Inverness | 25,651 | 25,779 | 128 | 0·5 |
| King's | 23,469 | 22,489 | — 980 | — 4·0 |
| Lunenburg | 28,583 | 31,075 | 2,492 | 8·7 |
| Pictou | 35,535 | 34,541 | — 994 | — 2·7 |
| Queen's | 10,577 | 10,610 | 33 | 0·3 |
| Richmond | 15,121 | 14,399 | — 722 | — 4·7 |
| Shelburne | 14,913 | 14,956 | 43 | 0·3 |
| Victoria | 12,470 | 12,432 | — 38 | — 0·3 |
| Yarmouth | 21,284 | 22,216 | 932 | 4·3 |
| **New Brunswick.** | | | | |
| Albert | 12,329 | 10,971 | —1,358 | —11·0 |
| Carleton | 23,265 | 22,529 | — 836 | — 3·6 |
| Charlotte | 26,087 | 23,752 | —2,335 | — 8·9 |
| Gloucester | 21,614 | 24,897 | 3,283 | 15·2 |
| Kent | 22,618 | 23,845 | 1,227 | 5·4 |
| King's | 25,617 | 23,087 | —2,530 | — 9·8 |
| Northumberland | 25,109 | 25,713 | 604 | 2·4 |
| Queen's | 14,107 | 12,152 | —1,865 | —13·3 |
| Restigouche | 7,058 | 8,308 | 1,250 | 17·7 |
| St. John (City) | 26,127 | 24,184 | —1,943 | — 7·4 |
| St. John (County) | 26,839 | 25,390 | —1,449 | — 5·4 |
| Sunbury | 6,651 | 5,762 | — 889 | —13·3 |
| Victoria | 15,686 | 18,217 | 2,531 | 16·1 |
| Westmorland | 37,719 | 41,477 | 3,758 | 9·9 |
| York | 30,397 | 30,979 | 582 | 1·9 |
| **P. E. Island.** | | | | |
| King's | 26,433 | 26,633 | 200 | 0·7 |
| Prince | 34,347 | 36,470 | 2,123 | 6·2 |
| Queen's | 48,111 | 45,975 | —2,136 | — 4·4 |

Now here we have the alarming fact that seventeen counties in the Maritime Provinces, eight in Nova Scotia, eight in New Brunswick and one in P. E. Island, HAVE NOT ONLY LOST ALL THEIR NATURAL INCREASE OF POPULATION, BUT HAVE ACTUALLY *FEWER PEOPLE THAN THEY HAD TEN YEARS AGO.

If the process continues it will take only a few years to depopulate them altogether.

But how about the Maritime Cities!!

Unfortunately their plight is if anything worse.

Turn again to the record. The census returns show the following as the result of the census in cities in the Maritime Provinces of 5,000 inhabitants in 1881 and 1891;

| | | | Increase or Decrease | |
|---|---|---|---|---|
| Cities. | 1891. | 1891. | Number. | Per Cent. |
| St. John, - - | 41,353 | 39,178 | —2,174 | |
| Halifax, - - | 36,100 | 38,556 | 2,456 | |
| Charlottetown, - | 11,485 | 11,374 | — 111 | |
| Moncton, - - | 5,032 | 8,765 | 3,733 | |
| Fredericton, - - | 6,218 | 6,502 | 284 | |
| Yarmouth, - - | 3.485 | 6,089 | 2,604 | |
| Truro, - - - | 3,461 | 5,102 | 1,641 | |
| Total, - - | 107,134 | 115,567 | | |

Now supposing the natural increase of population in these cities had been retained, how would their population have respectively stood in 1891:

| | 1881. Population | Natural increase 2 per ct. per year | Population as it should have increased. | Actual loss or gain in Population. |
|---|---|---|---|---|
| St. John, | 41,353 | 8,270 | 49,623 | —10,444 |
| Halifax, | 36,100 | 7,220 | 43,320 | — 4,764 |
| Charlottetown, | 11,485 | 2,297 | 13,782 | — 2,308 |
| Moncton, | 5,032 | 1,006 | 6,038 | + 2,727 |
| Fredericton, | 6,218 | 1,243 | 7,461 | — 959 |
| Yarmouth | 3,485 | 697 | 4,182 | + 1,907 |
| Truro, | 3,461 | 692 | 4,153 | + 947 |
| Total, | 107,134 | 21,425 | 128,559 | 12,992 |

Total population of the above seven cities as they would have been in 1891 if they had retained their natural increase, . - - - · · · · - · 128,559

Total population as shown by census returns, 1891, - 115,567

Actual loss in 10 years, - · - - - - · 12,992

## A SAMPLE NEW BRUNSWICK COUNTY.

Albert County, New Brunswick, is a striking illustration of the baneful effects of the National Policy. It is a county with a large sea-board, rich agricultural resources, fine stone quarries, unrivalled deposits of plaster, and ship-owners' investments. Here is the county's record until the two fiscal policies:

From 1871 to 1881 Albert County INCREASED under a low revenue tariff, 1,657.

From 1881 to 1891 Albert County DECREASED under a high protective tariff, 1,358.

In the past ten years the county has lost within 300 of its total gain of the ten years preceding.

# SHIPPING.

One of the great industries of the Maritime Provinces was its shipping. The following tables indicate its RISE, progress, and decadence.

Statement of the shipping of the Maritime Provinces for the years 1873, 1878 and 1893, as shown by the Marine and Fisheries Report, 1894, page cvi.:

|      | Nova Scotia. Tonnage. | New Brunswick. Tonnage. | P.E. Island. Tonnage. |
| ---- | --------------------- | ----------------------- | --------------------- |
| 1873 | 449,701               | 277,850                 | 38,918                |
| 1878 | 553,368               | 335,965                 | 54,250                |
| 1893 | 396,263               | 156,086                 | 20,970                |

From the foregoing table it appears that while the registered tonnage of the three Provinces in 1873 was as follows:

|                | Tons.   |
| -------------- | ------- |
| Nova Scotia    | 449,701 |
| New Brunswick  | 227,840 |
| P. E. Island   | 38,918  |
| Total,         | 716,469 tons. |

It had increased in the year 1878 to the following figures:

| | |
|---|---|
| Nova Scotia | 553,368 |
| New Brunswick | 335,965 |
| P. E. Island | 54,250 |
| Total | 943,783 tons. |

or an increase of 237,114 tons which, at the average value per ton estimated by the Marine Department of $30, make AN IN-CREASE in the value of the registered tonnage of $7,113,42o between the years 1873 and 1878.

The National Policy was introduced in 1879, and has continued in force ever since. The registered tonnage in 1893 was

| | |
|---|---|
| Nova Scotia | 396,268 |
| New Brunswick | 156,086 |
| P. E. Island | 20,970 |
| Total, | 573,319 tons, |

or a DECREASE OR LOSS of 370,264 tons, and at the same estimate of $30 per ton of $11,108,220.

It is contended that this deplorable decrease is not chargeable to the National Policy and certainly there were other causes which contributed to bring it about.

But while credit is taken to that Policy for every increase in the industries of the people, since it was introduced, it is well to call attention to the fact, that one of the chief industries and modes of investing their money of the people of the Maritime Provinces HAS ALARMINGLY DECREASED UNDER IT.

The money formerly invested in ships has been withdrawn or lost, and to a considerable extent that portion withdrawn has been invested in those FACTORIES or INDUSTRIES such as the SUGAR and COTTON FACTORIES which are not indigenous to the country but have been called into being and are maintained by the NATIONAL POLICY.

If instead of protecting by heavy taxation on the people the sugar and cotton industries, and so inducing capitalists to withdraw their capital from the natural industries of the country and invest it in these exotic manufactures, our people had been encouraged and induced in all legitimate ways, to change their wooden ships for iron and steel ships, as was done in Great Britain, we would not have had the deplorable record as shown above staring us in the face.

In the foregoing figures no reference has been made to shipbuilding.

The facts are as follows :

### NOVA SCOTIA BUILT.

| | No. of Vessels. | Tonnage. | | | |
|---|---|---|---|---|---|
| 1874 | 175 | 84,480 | Value at $40 per ton | $3,379,200 |
| 1878 | 167 | 49,784 | " " | 1,991,360 |
| 1893 | 111 | 15,089 | " " | 603,360 |

### NEW BRUNSWICK BUILT.

| | No. of Vessels. | Tonnage. | | | |
|---|---|---|---|---|---|
| 1874 | 90 | 42,027 | Value at $40 per ton, | $1,681,080 |
| 1878 | 56 | 27,368 | " " | 1,094,720 |
| 1893 | 119 | 2,819 | " " | 112,760 |

### PRINCE EDWARD ISLAND BUILT.

| | No of Vessels. | Tonnage. | | | |
|---|---|---|---|---|---|
| 1874 | 88 | 24,634 | Value at $40 per ton, | $ 985,360 |
| 1878 | 28 | 10,348 | " " | 415,280 |
| 1893 | 3 | 634 | " " | 25,360 |

The industry is practically extinct.

### SEA-GOING SHIPPING.

Pardonable pride is exhibited by Canadians from time to time in pointing to the fact that Canada is the Fifth mercantile power in the world.

Statistics show however that the National Policy or high taxation is "getting in its work" in this direction as well as in others.

"Protection" as Sir Charles Tupper once observed before he became a pervert from Free Trade principles, "has swept the American Flag from the sea." Let us in Canada beware lest our continuance in maintaining the odious system may produce the same results.

To day of the ocean borne freight to and from Canada, only about 20 is carried in Canadian bottoms, while 80 is carried in British and Foreign ships.

Below we give a table from Trade and navigation returns for 1894 p. 576, showing the SEAGOING VESSELS inwards and outwards during the year ending June 30, 1893.

## TOTAL SEA-GOING VESSELS, Inwards and Outwards, 1893.

| | Tons Register. | Quantity of Freight. Tons weight. | Crew, Number |
|---|---|---|---|
| British, | 3,780,915 | 1,698,734 | 106,861 |
| Canadian, | 2,189,725 | 805,741 | 109,952 |
| Foreign, | 4,637,771 | 1,086,056 | 200,822 |
| | 10,608,611 | 3,590,531 | 417,625 |

This shows that of 10,608,611 tons shipping employed in carrying the 3,590,531 tons weight of freight to and from Canada only about one-fifth is Canadian. Of the 417,635 men employed only 109,952 are employed in Canadian ships.

Nearly 80 p.c. of the profits of Canada's seagoing carrying trade goes to Foreigners and others outside of Canada. If we rejoice that Canada's exports have increased our joy must be tempered with the knowledge, that we employ Foreign bottoms to carry them away and that foreigners enjoy the profits of the carriage.

In 1878, matters were not so bad. The statistical abstract p. 625, shows that in that year, the seagoing shipping entered and cleared at Canadian Ports with cargo and in Ballast was as follows :

| | BRITISH. Tons Register. | CANADIAN. Tons Register. | FOREIGN. Tons Register. | Total Tonnage |
|---|---|---|---|---|
| 1878 | 2,294,688 | 1,928,531 | 2,461,165 | 6,684,384 |

This shows that in 1878 of the total tonnage engaged about 29 p.c. was Canadian. Instead of increasing,our relative proportion in 1893 was reduced to 20 p. c.

The number of crews employed that year is not given in the "Statistical Report."

Compare the foregoing tables and facts with similar tables as regards British shipping.

The Registered tonnage of Great Britain (see Statesman's year Book) was in 1850, 3,096,000 ; 1860, 4,325,000 ; 1880, 6,236,-000 ; 1092, 8,644,754.

The greatest part of the entire international trade of the world is conducted in British bottoms.

## HALIFAX AS A WINTER PORT.

The Tories wish to make the Haligonians believe they have built up Halifax as the winter port in Canada and diverted traffic from American ports. But this is not true. In 1893 the ocean borne tonnage over the I. C. R. to and from Halifax was only 19,714 tons as against 18,354 tons in 1878, a year of depression. Six years ago (in 1888) the ocean borne tonnage was nearly three times as large as in 1893. and in 1883 (ten years before) it was 32,786 tons as against 19,714 tons in 1893. What do these statistics show ? That the N. P. has dwarfed the natural growth of Halifax as a winter port and crippled the earning ability of the Intercolonial Railway.

## COTTON MILLS AND SUGAR REFINERIES.

Now as to these COTTON AND SUGAR MILLS and the monies invested in them, let us look at the census returns.

New Brunswick had in 1891 five mills, viz., St. Croix, Courtenay Bay, Parks, Moncton, and Marysville.

The capital invested in them in Land, Buildings, Machinery and working capital, $2,733,000.

They employed 625 men, 853 women, 147 boys under 16, 127 girls. Total hands, 1752.

They paid out in wages $498,000 or $284 each employee. Nova Scotia had in 1891 two mills, one in Halifax and one in Windsor had a total capital in land, $21,114, buildings, $111,883, machinery, $283,988, working capital, $158,800, making in all $575,785.

They employed 184 men, 190 women, 56 boys, 33 girls, total 463. To whom were paid $90,753, wages yearly or $196 per head.

What returns were made on the capital. The Marysville Cotton Factory is a private enterprise owned and run under very exceptional circumstances by a man of indomitable energy, Mr. ALEX. GIBSON. He pays NO TAXES, PAYS nothing for fuel, using the refuse of his saw mills therefor and manages himself.

Such a mill ought to pay a return and would no doubt do so under any Government Policy. When unrestricted receprocity was being discussed, Mr. Gibson felt so sure of his ability to compete with the American manufacturer that he is reported to have expressed himself as willing to abandon Protection if he could gain access for his wares to the American market.

The history of the other mills is pretty much the same. The mills were bonded to raise money to carry on their business.

Restricted to a small market in Canada fiercely competing in that market with each other and the many other Canadian mills, the production far exceeded the demand, the prices fell, the mills closed down, the mortgagees foreclosed, the mills were sold and the result was that the original capitalists lost the mills and EVERY DOLLAR OF THEIR CAPITAL INVESTED IN THEM and went for years without any dividend or return.

In the case of the Moncton Mills the original shareholders got back some 17 or 20 cents on the dollar of their investment. To-day they are all (excepting Gibsons) in a HUGE COM-BINE, governed by a central committee at Montreal, sometimes shut down, other times running on part time, and entirely managed in the interests of the monopolists. The Protective Tariff permits and enables this combine, all competition being done away with and foreign competition prohibited by the Tariff, to charge just such prices as the monopolists please, limited only by the prices charged for foreign goods after paying the duties.

## SUGAR.

Great credit is claimed by the Protectionists for having taken off the duties upon sugar some years ago, and as they say reduced the TAXATION OF THE PEOPLE SOME THREE AND A HALF MILLIONS OF DOLLARS YEARLY.

Mr. Foster in his Budget speech last year said :—

" The duties on glass have been reduced ; the duties on salt " have been reduced one half and more than all, three years ago "the duty on raw sugar was completely taken off, REMITTING "TAXATION to the amount that had formerly been collected."

This claim explicitly admits that the duties they exacted on sugar for YEARS WERE TAXES PAID BY THE PEOPLE. This was formerly denied. Its admission is most important not only as regards sugar but all other articles taxed by duties.

It must not be forgotten that these sugar taxes were only removed when the Government was forced to do so by the action of the United States Government in reducing the sugar duties there.

All sugar duties however are not removed, sixty-four one-hundredths, or practically $\frac{2}{3}$ of a cent per lb. is still exacted on Refined Sugar.

This gives a substantial protection to the sugar refiners, who importing the raw sugar FREE, refine it, sell it to the consumer and make him pay TO THEM, in INCREASED PRICE, the duty of $\frac{2}{3}$ of a cent. per lb. which he would have paid into the Treasury, if he imported his sugar. In this way the consumer pays an enormous tax upon sugar. What it amounts to cannot be estimated with mathematical accuracy, because it is not known whether the refiner charges the consumer with the full protection of sixty-four one-hundredths or $\frac{2}{3}$ of a cent per lb. on every pound consumed. If he does the tax the sugar consumer paid would amount to over $1,500,000. But if he only paid $\frac{2}{3}$ of that protective tax, it would reach the respectable sum of over one million dollars. All of which goes into the pockets of the sugar refiners.

In 1893 WE IMPORTED 1,651,670 LBS. REFINED SUGAR and the duty of eight-tenths of a cent. per lb. gave the revenue about $9,000. In the same year WE IMPORTED 245 MILLION POUNDS OF RAW SUGAR.

Being FREE the revenue got NOTHING. On its manufactured product there then was a duty of eight-tenths of a cent, now sixty-four—one-hundredths When this 245 million pounds raw sugar were manufactured into refined sugar and sold to the consumer, does the reader imagine the refiner made him a PRESENT OF THE AMOUNT OF HIS PROTECTION. The idea is absurd. Sugar refiners are like all other men. They will charge all they can get and when they have a protection of ⅔ of a cent, a lb. they charge that to the consumer or just so much short of it as enables them to undersell foreign sugars, and whether that is ¾. ⅔ or ½ of this protection the result is very large. Now the estimate of the quantity of refined sugar consumed in Canada yearly is from 250 to 300 millions pounds, on the basis of 250 millions pounds of consumption the ⅔ cent. per lb. duty, would leave the snug sum of $1,600,000 as paid by the consumer of sugar to the refiner. Whileonly $9,000 was paid into the Treasury.

But the N. P. man points to the price of sugar in New York as being higher than sugar in Montreal.

Why ! Because the America Tariff exacts a tax of 40 p.c. on the cost alike of RAW and REFINED SUGAR.—This is equal to nearly a cént a lb. The Treasury gets the benefit of all this tax and has an additional tax of ¼ cent, per lb. on refined sugar as protection to the refiners, equal to 12½ cents per 100 lbs.

Our tariff admits raw sugar free and imposes a tax of 64 cents. per 100 lbs. on refined.

Thus the Canadian refiner has 51½ cents per 100 lbs greater protection than the American.

The New York refiner pays including the duty for his raw sugar 3 cents and sells granulated for 3¾ per lb.

The Canadian gets his raw sugar free and charges 3 3-8 for his granulated.

He therefor makes ½ cent a lb. or $1.50 a barrel more for his sugar than the American refiner for his.

The Canadian Treasury GETS NOTHING. If the refiner says he does not charge the duty why keep it on.

The value of the products of these refineries by the census of 1891 was $17,000,000.

If we were allowed to import our sugar free from England
we would save just ⅛ of that amount being the difference between the cost of sugar imported from England and that
bought in Canada.

That would mean $2,125,000. If the duty makes no differ-
ence in the price charged by the refiner, we say take it off and
give the people a present of $2,000,000.

## · THE RICE QUESTION.

By a similar leger-de-main the people are compelled to pay
about $300,000 yearly in the shape of taxes upon rice while only
about $50,000 finds its way into the Treasury.

The feat is worked in this way:—

Cleaned rice pays a duty of 1¼ cents per lb; uncleaned pays
about ¼ of a cent per lb. There is consequently a protection
of 1 cent a lb. given to those who import the paddy or uncleaned
rice, and hull and clean it.

The Trade and Nav. Returns for 1894 p. 16 show that in the
year 1893-4 there was imported over 3½ millions lbs of cleaned
rice ,which paid a duty to the treasury of about $44,000. While
of uncleaned rice there was imported close on 23,000,000 lbs
which only paid about $53,000 to the treasury. This 23,000,000
lbs of uncleaned rice made about 22,000,000 lbs when cleaned
ready for sale.

The cleaner being protected one cent a lb would of course
charge that or nearly all to the consumer to whom he sold the
rice.

The consumer therefore paid the tax of 1¼ cents for each lb. of
rice he consumed, but he paid ¼ cent each lb. or in all $53,000 to
the treasury while he paid 1 cent per lb, or $220,000 to the cleaner.

In this way out of every $5 of taxes the consumer paid, the
treasury got $1 and the manufacturer $4.

Last session Mr. Foster tried to remedy this gross injustice
and when he introduced his new tariff, he proposed to reduce the
duty on cleaned rice and raise it on unhulled, so that the
treasury might receive more of the taxes paid by the rice consumers.

The rice cleaners however sent a deputation to the capital,
took the Finance Minister by the throat and made him abandon
his reform, and leave the consumer at the mercy of the cleaner of
rice. It was discovered that the proposed reform was a "clerical
error" and the tariff was restored to what it had originally
been.

## THE CORDAGE COMBINE.

The customs tax is 1¼ per lb., and 10 per
about 2½ cents a pound. This to a maritime pec
most odious impositions of the National Policy
most grievous injustice.

The monopoly of Canada enjoyed by "
Cordage Company " is almost complete.

Canada has been handed over to the tender mei
less corporation, bound hand and foot, and pays
IN HUNDREDS OF THOUSANDS OF DOLLA
cornage is practically excluded by a duty of a :
cents a pound.

The smaller rope factories were bought up b
bine, their doors closed, their workmen turned
proprietors paid THOUSANDS A YEAR to
enjoy themselves.

The rope factories in St. John and Qnebec ai

Having silenced in this way Cenadian comp
foreign competition excluded by the tariff, the Co
Co., with Mr. John F. Stairs, M. P. for Halifax, a
(and it need hardly be said an out-and-out sup|
P.) proceeds to recoup its expenditure in buyin
and to build up collossal fortunes for the
monopolies by fleecing the Canadian Consumer

The 2 1·6 cents duty per pound, payable upoi
imported, is not paid into the Treasury by tho
because practically foreign rope is excluded.

The consumer is bound to buy the Canadian

He pays the tax of 2 1-6 cents a pound, or
right, but he pays it to Mr. John F. Stairs, M
monopolists, and not to the Treasury.

So complete is the monopoly that the Att
Nova Scotia publicly stated that he would be v
" weight in solid silver for every inch of ro
bought, or compelled to be bought, from this si:
the Dominion of Canada."

But this combine, when it sells its rope in ]
St. Pierre, has to sell it in competition with ro
elsewhere, and actually sells it, from 1 1-2 to
pound than it sells the same article to Canadi;

This is an intolerable outrage sanctioned,
maintained by the National Policy.

Some kinds of cordage, not manufactur
bine is imported still, and the revenue ieceive|
$14,000 in duty on it. But rope is monopolized

# KEROSENE OIL.

No duty is more unjust, unfair or discriminating than that charged upon kerosene oil.

Its history is, that somewhere about the year 1868 a customs duty of 15 cents a gallon and an excise duty were levied on kerosene oil.

In 1877 the excise duty was removed, and the customs duty reduced to 6 cents per wine gallon.

When the imperial gallon was adopted this duty was increased to 7 1-5 cents and so remained until 1894, when after a very vigorous fight the Liberals in Parliament, headed by Mr. Davies, succeeded in forcing a slight reduction of 1 1-5 cents, making the present duty 6 cents per imperial gallon.

But the iniquity of this tax can be properly appreciated only by remembering that when the duty was left at 6 cents a wine gallon in 1877, the price of American oil of the same quality as that now imported, was 20 cents per gallon, which made the then duty about 30 per cent. Of late years the price has fallen to $3\frac{1}{2}$ cents per wine gallon, while the duty remains the same at 6 cents —equivalent to nearly 150 per cent.

Many invoices of imported oil were read in Parliament last session.

One importation to St. John, N. B., March, 1894: Two tanks oil, invoice $396; **Quantity, 10,908 gallons; Duty paid, $785, almost 200 Per Cent.**

Another invoice about same date: Quantity, 9,643 gallons; invoice cost, $405; Duty paid, $694.

Last November (1894) the Eastern Oil Co. produced an invoice of oil imported into St. John under the present tariff: Invoice cost, 721; duty, $1,029—equal to nearly 150 per cent.

The trade and Navigation Returns for 1894 show that in that year there was imported into Canada, 5,958,368 gallons, value $436,476, on which duty was paid to the amount of $430,564.77, or almost **100 Per Cent.**

But that this is unjustly levied can be seen from the following table:

| | Quantity, Galls. | Value. | Duty. | Per Centage |
|---|---|---|---|---|
| Ontario, | 2,064,578 | $153 797 | $148,652 | 96·6 |
| Quebec, | 783,858 | 52,655 | 56.437 | 107·1 |
| Nova Scotia, | 1,024,622 | 59,583 | 73.772 | 123·7 |
| New Brunswick, | 1,010,322 | 55,984 | 72,743 | 130·3 |
| P. E. Island, | 255,006 | 11,544 | 18,360 | 158 2 |
| Manitoba, | 397,113 | 20.263 | 28,600 | 141·1 |
| British Columbia, | 442,203 | 83,416 | 31,818 | 38·1 |
| Northwest Ter, | 2.481 | 450 | 178 | 39·5 |
| | 5,980,183 | $437,692 | $430,564 | 98·3 |

Now this unjust duty is maintained ostensibly to protect an Ontario Industry which gives employment a; shown by the census returns vol. 3 p. 231 to 276 persons.

The statistical abstract for 1894, p. 379 shows the quantity of CANADIAN OIL consumed in Canada in 1893 to have been 10,683,806 gallons, as against 6,249,946 gallons of American oil.

On this latter duties were paid into the Treasury amounting to about $430,000. An amount equivalent to that duty or more must have been paid the Canadian oil refiner.

The result was that the Canadian consumer paid into the Treasury in taxes on the Canadian oil he consumed $430,000 and on the 10½ million gallons of CANADIAN OIL he paid the Canadian manufacturer $760,000 or nearly $2 for every $1 paid paid into the Treasury.

Supposing the Canadian manufacturer let the consumer off one-half the tax, he would still have paid in taxes on oil not $1 of which went to the Treasury, nearly $400,000.

All this to give employment to 260 men.

## GOODS CHEAP AS EVER ! !

But the argument is advanced by Tory speakers that GOODS ARE AS CHEAP IN CANADA AS EVER THEY WERE.

Even if this statement was correct it is entirely beside the question.

That question simply is *are goods as cheap as they ought to be and as they would be if the protective duties were removed ?*

What are the facts. They are that owing to improved machinery, cheap raw products, cheap food, etc. Goods are now and have been for some years manufactured and sold in England cheaper than ever before.

Remember the farmer does not now receive anything like as much for his products as he used to. Look at the figures.

|  | | 1884 | 1894 |
|---|---|---|---|
| Wheat, per bushel, | - | 80 cts. | 55 cts. |
| Barley, " | - | 53 " | 38 " |
| Oats, " | - | 33 " | 28 " |
| Hay, per ton, | - | $9.50 | $7.50 |

It is manifest, therefore, if the farmer gets so much less for his produce and has to pay the old prices for the goods he requires to buy, he must be so much the worse off.

Now the following table, reproduced from the Commercial Bulletin, shows the exports and selling values of the great staple goods in England in 1874, 1884, and 1894:

## EXPORTS FROM GREAT BRITAIN.

| Cotton Yarns (lbs.) | Percentage of increase or decrease. | Value. | Percentage of increas or decrease. |
|---|---|---|---|
| 1874 | 220,599,074 | | £14,516,093 stg. | |
| 1884 | 271,077,900 | +18·6 | 13,811,767 | — 4·8 |
| 1894 | 236,198,500 | —12·8 | 9,289,078 | —32·7 |
| Cotton Fabrics (yds). | | | |
| 1874 | 3,603,348,527 | | £55,014,066 | |
| 1884 | 4,417,481,000 | +22·6 | 51,061,408 | — 7·18 |
| 1894 | 5,312,753,900 | +20·2 | 50,223,291 | — 1·6 |
| Linens (yds.) | | | |
| 1874 | 190,409,712 | | £6,173,255 | |
| 1884 | 150,672,700 | —20·8 | 4,149,830 | —32.7 |
| 1894 | 152,069,700 | + 0·93 | 3,273,448 | —21·1 |
| Iron and Steel Manufactures. | | | |
| 1874 | 2,487,162 (tons) | | £31,225,380 | |
| 1884 | 3,496,352 | +40.ö | 24,487,669 | —21·6 |
| 1894 | 2,656,125 | —24. | 18,731,140 | —23·5 |

These figures in themselves speak volumes. In *cotton yarns* they show an increase in quantity produced in 1884 over 1874 of 18% while the *increased quantity* was sold at 4% *less*. In 94, 12% less *in quantity* was produced, but it sold for 32.7 p. c. or nearly one-third *less in price* than in 1884.

In *Cotton Fabrics*, the year 1884 produced 22·6% more than 1874, yet the product sold for 7.18 per cent *less price* showing a cheapening of nearly 30 per cent in ten years.

1894 showed astill further increase of 20 per cent *in quantity* produced while it sold for 1 per cent *less price*.

The same story is told in Linens. 1884 produced 20 per cent less in quantity than 1874, but sold for 32 per cent *less price*, while 1894 producing nearly 1 per cent more sold for 21 per cent *less*.

In Iron and Steel the results are more wonderful, the year 1884 produced 40 per cent more quantity than 1874 and England sold it to her customers 21 per cent *less than she sold the smaller production of 1874.* The year 1894 produced 24 per cent. less quantity and England sold it 23 per cent. *less than she sold her 1884 product.*

## COTTON AND COTTON GOODS ! !

But apart from the above tables let us look at the facts.

Mr. Edgar stated in the House of Commons and the correctness of his statements has never been challenged, that the raw cotton fell in cost between 1890 and 1893, 1 cent 6 mills a pound. This, on the enormous quantity imported of about 40 millions of pounds, amounted alone to a profit of $660,000. The wages of the operatives were not raised and the prices charged to the consumer instead of being lowered were raised from 10 to 25 per cent. during those three years. But the dividends and the reserve funds set apart by the companies were raised.

Mr. Edgar further stated that 13 million dollars worth of cotton is manufactured by the Canadian Cotton Companies, and that the duty paid by the importers last year, on all cotton goods brought into the country was a trifle over 28 per cent. Supposing there was no other profit on that $13,000,000 than the 28 per cent. paid by the actual importers, who, paid that in addition to the freight and profits paid to 'the' English manufacturer of cotton goods,that would make a sum of $3,640,000 paid by the people to the Combine, under the protection given by the Tariff.

In other words, on the $4,500,600 worth imported a tax of $1,260,000 is paid, which goes into the treasury, and on the $13,000,000 worth of cottons manufactured, an equivalent tax of $3,640,000 is paid, which goes into the coffers of the combines.

Take the history of these Combines to see how the people are fleeced and the facts hidden from them. In 1892 the Dominion Cotton Co. one of the combines which controls 11 mills of the country, had a Capital of $1,500,000. They decided to double that Capital. They issued the new stock to themselves. They only paid of the new stock 10 per cent, or $150,000 and the balance of $1,350,000 was watered. On April 14th 1893 the annual report of that Company was published. It stated that the earnings for that year were about 20 per cent on the capital of $3,000,600 but as on the last $1,500,000 the shareholders only paid 10 per cent, or $150,000 while the Company paid a profit of 10 per cent on the whole 1½ millions, these gentlemen *actually received 200 per cent* on all the money they paid in.

# INCREASED DUTIES ON DRY GOODS.

The National Policy has imposed very heavy duties on dry goods. Careful examination by large importers has shown that the average duty on dry goods is about 33 per cent. against 17½ per cent. under the Liberal Government. But many articles in common use by the middle and poorer classes pay very much higher duties. Cloth, of which the clothing of working people is largely made, has been taxed 40, 50, and even 60 per cent. The consumer has to pay not only the increased duty, but a good deal more, as will be seen by the following calculation :

Comparison of cost—$100 worth of Dry Goods.

UNDER LIBERAL TARIFF.

| | |
|---|---|
| Cost of goods in England, | $100.00 |
| Importation, Freight, Insurance, etc., 8 p. c., | 8.00 |
| Duty, 17½ p. c., | 17.50 |
| Cost to importer, | $125 50 |
| Wholesaler's profit, 15 p. c., | 18.82 |
| Cost to retailer, | $144.32 |
| Retailer's profit, 25 p. c., | 36.08 |
| Cost to consumer, | $180.40 |

Thus even under the Liberal tariff it cast $80 to place $100 worth of goods from England in the hands of the consumer. Now let us make a similar calculation under the National Policy, with average duty on dry goods 33 per cent.

UNDER TORY TARIFF.

| | |
|---|---|
| Cost of dry goods in England | $100.00 |
| Cost of importation | 8.00 |
| Duty, 33 p. c. | 33.00 |
| Cost to importer, | $141.00 |
| Wholesaler's profit 15 p. c., | 21.15 |
| Cost to retailer, | $162.15 |
| Retailer's profit, 25 p. c. | 40.51 |
| Cost to consumer, | $202.65 |

| | |
|---|---|
| Cost of $100 worth of goods under Liberal tariff, | $ 180.40 |
| Cost of $100 worth of goods under National Policy, | 202.65 |
| Increased cost to consumer, | $ 22.25 |

A similar calculation applied to a parcel of cloth used for clothing, and paying 60 per cent. duty, would be as follows:

| | |
|---|---:|
| Cost of goods, | $ 100.00 |
| Cost of importation, | 18.00 |
| Duty 60 per cent., | 60.00 |
| Cost to importer, | $ 168.00 |
| Wholesaler's profit, 15 p. c., | 25.20 |
| Cost to retailer, | $ 193.20 |
| Retailer's profit, 25 p. c., | 48.30 |
| Cost to consumer, | $ 241.50 |

Cost of $100 worth of goods under Liberal tariff,    $ 180.40
Cost of $100 worth of goods under National Policy,    241.50

Increased cost to consumer,    $ 61.10

Under the system of an ad valorem and specific duties there are many cases in which articles of dry good are taxed as high as 60 per cent.

## THE IRON DUTIES.

The positive harmfulness of protection is well illustrated by the history of Canada's desperate efforts to tax her iron industry into greatness. All she has succeeded in doing has been to tax herself very nearly to death. In the low tariff period from 1867 to 1879 pig iron was free while a 5 per cent. duty only, was imposed upon bar and rod iron. Coal was free too. Coal and iron are raw materials of every manufacture and by making them as cheap as possible the low tariff governments gave encouragement to the establishment of manufactures. Agricultural implement factories in particular sprang up here and there, and foundries and rolling mills began to make their appearance. Unfortunately for Canada a Protectionist Government came into power in 1878, and in overhauling the tariff, duties of $2 per ton were placed on pig iron, 17½ per cent on bar iron, and in proportion, on other forms of iron, or manufactures of it. But it is the fate of a protective duty to go on enlarging itself until it bursts. In 1883 the duty was reinforced by a bounty of $1.50 per ton. As the development of the iron industry still failed to satisfy the Government, Sir Charles Tupper, in 1887 resolved on drastic measures, and brought down to the house a new iron schedule. By it pig was taxed $4 per ton, (or $4.50 per per long ton in which form pig iron is bought); puddled bars $9 per ton; bar iron $13 per ton; plate iron $13 per ton; cast iron pipe $12 per ton; hoop iron $13 per ton, and everything else in proportion. At the same time the bounty was reduced to $1 per ton.

## TUPPER'S PROMISES.

This new tariff, Sir Charles Tupper assured the House, was going to do the trick. He predicted that the iron industry which would spring up in consequence would furnish employment to "an army of men, numbering at least twenty thousand, increasing our population from 80,000 to 100,000 souls, and affording the means of supporting them in comfort and prosperity." He declared that were we to manufacture all the iron and steel articles imported, "and there is no reason why we should not steadily progress to that point, the populalation I have mentioned of 100,000 souls, would be no less than trebled." He prophesied that blast furnaces would be called into existence in Carleton (N. B.), British Columbia, Manitoba, Cobourg, Kingston and Weller's Bay. All this was to be done without the cost of iron and steel being increased to the consumer.

How different was the realization! The first effect of the tariff was to very nearly double the price of every piece of hardware, from a ten-penny nail up. It in the course of a year or so all but wiped out the important iron and hardware importing business of the country. This prejudically affected the shipping interests, and the profits of the steamship lines began to decrease until they disappeared altogether. One of the chief lines of steamers is now in liquidation largely as the result of this attempt to force these blast furnaces into existence. By affecting the shipping interests it added to the cost of transportation of wheat to Great Britain and thus reduced the farmers' profits on grain. Thus this iron schedule can account these amoung its accomplishments: *It has increased to the Canadian consumer the price of every article in the manufacture of which iron enters, from 50 to 100 per cent., thus adding not less than three or four million dollars per year to the taxation borne by the Canadian people;* it has ruined the iron and hardware importing houses, it has burdened the manufacturers who use iron, it has seriously

### INJURED CANADA'S SHIPPING INTERESTS,

and it has lessened the price of every bushel of Canadian wheat exported.

And unfortunately for the protectionist apologist, he cannot say in reply: "But, is not all this more than compensated for by the blast furnaces which nightly crimson the sky at Carleton County, Welle.'s Bay, Cobourg, Kingston, Manitoba and British Columbia, by the 100,000 souls maintained in 'comfort and prosperity?' If all that Sir Charles predicted in the way of development had come to pass the game would still have been too dear for the candle. But not even one of George Johnson's lynx-eyed enumerators could discover the

100,000 people or the blast furnaces. They never materialized and Sir Charles' prediction was put on the shelf along side of his other famous prophesy made in 1879, that in fifteen years the Canadian Northwest would be exporting 640,000,000 bushels of wheat annually.

## THE IRONMASTERS' MONOPOLY.

The iron duties worked to the enrichment of one class—the home makers of hardware. It did not greatly assist the production of pig iron, which was nominally its object. For this there was a very good reason. The protectionists who in selling want to have the people obliged, under penalty of fine, to buy from them at their own price, are not in buying ignorant of the virtues of Free Trade. The rolling mill men, the nail combinesters, the makers of tubings, etc., saw clearly enough that the effect of such a tariff as that proposed would be to greatly *increase the price of that which they had to sell;* but they saw with equal clearness that if the *cost of their iron* were increased their position would not be improved. They therefore journeyed to Ottawa, and as gratitude for past favors, as well as a lively expectation of further favors to come, impelled the Government to treat them with marked consideration, they got what they wanted.

A clause was inserted in the schedule which while it in no degree lessened the effect of the duties, *deprived the producers of pig iron of most of the benefits they anticipated.* The duty on scrap iron was left at $2 per ton. In consequence, *the rolling mills in place of using iron made from Canadian pig imported scrap from the ends of the earth and used it in preference.* We have the authority of Mr. Foster, the Finance Minister, for saying that in consequence *of this gross discrimination no bar iron was made in Canada from Canadian puddled bars.* The manufacturers of hardware bought their raw material almost at free trade prices, and they sold their *output at the highest point the extreme tariff permitted.* To make sure that they should get every cent possible from this condition of affairs, which they doubtless knew was too good to last, they formed a series of combines to regulate prices, and bull-doze wholesalers from any attempt at importation. These combines, as they existed a year or so ago, were made up as follows:

## FOSTERED COMBINES.

Wire nail combine; Pillow & Hersey, Montreal; Peck, Benny & Co Montreal; Montreal Rolling Mills Co.; Dominion Wire Manufacturing Company; the Ontario Tack Company, Hamilton; the Ontario Lead Pipe and Barbed Wire Company, Toronto; the Ontario Bolt and Forge Co , Swansea; Parmenter & Bullock, Gananoque.

Canadian Tack Combine: Pillow & Hersey, Montreal Rolling Mills, Peck, Benny & Co , the Ontario Tack Company.

Horse shoe Combine: Pillow & Hersey, Abbott & Co., Peck, Benny & Co.,Montreal Rolling Mills.

Pressed Wrought Spike Combine: Peck, Benny & Co.,Pillow & Hersey, Abbott & Co., Montreal Rolling Mills, Abbott & Co., the Ontario Forge & Bolt Co.

Bar Iron Combine: Pillow & Hersey Company, Abbott & Co., Montreal Rolling Mills, Peck, Benny & Co.

The above list gives a very good idea of all those who profited by the enormous addition to the public taxation made by Sir Charles Tupper while laboring under the excitement of a prophetic spell.

## ENORMOUS PROTECTION.

So outrageous was this schedule that the Government was obliged at the session of 1894 to amend it By the new tariff then adopted, pig iron secured a duty of $4 and a bounty of $2 per ton, making the total protection $6 on the net ton; the duty on scrap was raised to $3 per ton, for the remainder of 1894, and to $4 per tor begiι ning January 1st, 1895: the bar iron duty was reduced from $13 to $10 per ton; puddled bars reduced from $9 to $5, and the other iron and steel duties equalized- This is a much more symmetrical schedule than the one it replaced,*but it will fail almost as lamentably in its attempt, to give employment in the iron industry to 20,000 men. Iron was cheapened so greatly during the last few years that despite the excessive protection,of $6 per ton, Canadian iron cannot hold its own let alone supplant the imported article.* In Montreal Scotch iron is very largely used, though American is beginning to get a strong footing; but in Ontario *American iron is almost exclusively employed in manufactures. It can be bought in Pennsylvania and laid down in Toronto with all charges paid* for less than would have to be paid there for the Canadian article. Is it not therefore as clear as that two and two make four that the effect of this duty is to handicap every Ontario manufacturer to the extent of $4.48—the amount of the duty—on every long ton of iron he possesses. The American manufacturer gets his iron from $4 to $5 a ton cheaper; his coal costs him 60c. a ton less, and in consequence he can manufacture much cheaper than can his Canadian rival The latter finds it difficult to compete in the Canadian markets notwithstanding the *excessive duties* on manufactures of iron; and when it comes to exporting he would not be in it for a single second had the Government not granted him relief by a device which illustrates the uselessness and costliness of Protection. By an Order-in-Council passed last fall, the Canadian manufacturer can recover on exported goods 99 per cent. of the duties paid for raw material. The Government in making such a regulation destroyed completely its own theory that the protective duty does not add to the cost of the goods, and they dealt a deadly blow as well at the native iron industry, the encouragemene of which has been the ostensible object of the legislation of the past 16 years. Mr. Geo E. Drummond, of Montreal. at the last meeting of the Quebec Mining Association, said that the "way in which this enactment is framed, and the manner in which it works are most detrimental to the development of the Canadian iron industry in its broadest sense." He said, furthermore, that it "simply serves to nullify the protection and encouragement to the Canadian iron industry, granted by the Dominion Government itself at the last session of Parliament."

## THE CONSUMER FLEECED.

While the manufacturer is thus handicapped, the consumer of iron articles is being unmercifully fleeced. The duties collected on iron and steel, and manufactures of same last year, 1894, were only about $100,000 short of $3,000,000. The consumer is therefore between the upper and the nether millstone, the Customs tax grinding above, the manufacturer below. The sum of about $3,000,000 ground out of him into the Treasury gives but a faint idea of what is squeezed out of him by the iron combines and trusts The latter must amount at the lowest figure to another $3,000,000.

To sum up, we have been trying for sixteen years to develop the Canadian iron industry by taxing foreign iron. During the last eight years of this period we have had excessively high duties on iron, and manufactures of iron, with the further assistance of a bounty. The only results have been to bleed the general consumer of millions of dollars, to handicap the manufacturer, and to destroy our importing and shipping interests, while the native pig iron industry is no further ahead than it probably would have been under free trade conditions. All this disturbance of normal trade conditions; all this destruction of genuine industries, all this piling on of taxes has been for the benefit of the congeries of combines which are in their own way useful to the Government at election times, by supplying not only generous donations to the campaign fund but a treasurer to administer it as well.

The iron duties are on the Liberal list. They will have to go.

# THE COAL DUTY.

Conservatives have said much about the value of protection to the coal trade. In nothing has the National Policy been a greater failure than in its effect on the coal trade. What the Nova Scotia coal miners were led to expect in 1878 was the control of the Canadian market, and the exclusion of imported coal, especially American. The great coal consuming province of Ontario was the particular market that was to be given to the miners. All these great expectations have been dissappointed. Excepting a very small quantity carried by the railways for their own use, in the eastern part of the Province, Nova Scotia has sent no coal to Ontario. American coal instead of being shut out, has come in more largely than ever. There has been an increase in the Nova Scotia coal trade, but only such as would probably have occurred if there had been no duty.

The record of the Conservatives on the coal question has been a very tortuous one. In 1878 one of their great cries was that they wanted reciprocity in coal and would get it. In the National Policy of 1879 they included a standing offer of free coal to the Americans. After a little while the mine managers of Nova Scotia (nearly all Conservatives) began to preach a different doctrine. They said they could not stand reciprocity in coal.

They declared that the admission of American coal would ruin them. Coal was taken out of the standing offer. For years the cry was that if coal was made free the Nova Scotia mines would have to close. This was notably the cry at the general election of March, 1891, when both the Tuppers, senior and junior, made speeches on these lines which had much influence in the mining districts. Official records now show that at that very time, while this cry was being raised in mining districts to influence the votes of miners, there was on file at Washington a letter from Sir John Macdonald offering to make coal free if the Americans would do the same. Here is a copy of the letter:

LES ROCHERS,
ST. PATRICK,
RIVIERE DU LOUP.

*Private*

July 30, 1890.

MY DEAR SIR,—In answer to your esteemed note of this day, I desire to say that I am fully assured that the Parliament of Canada will be ready to take off all Customs duty on coal, ores and lumber imported from the United States, whenever Congress makes those articles free of duty.

The Canadian Government has already authorized Sir Julian Pauncefote to state to the American Government that they will be prepared to take off the export duty on logs whenever Canadian lumber is admitted into the United States market at a reduced rate of $1.50 per thousand, board measure.

You are at liberty to show this to such members of Congress or the Government as you please. It should not, for obvious reasons, be published in the press or quoted in Congress.

In the U. S. Tariff Act provision might be made for the making the above-mentioned articles free whenever and so soon as they are made free by the Canadian Parliament.

I remain, my dear Sir,
Faithfully yours.
JOHN A MACDONALD.

S. J. RITCHIE, ESQ.

This letter, although marked "Private," was an official offer to the United States Government and was used as such. It became public by being placed on the files of a committee of the United States Congress, which had the tariff question under consideration. To tell the Nova Scotia miners that the Liberal policy of reciprocity in coal would close the mines, and to carry on negotiations at the same time to bring about just such a policy, was a piece of political juggling which an honorable government would hardly care to undertake. But the Ottawa Government were quite equal to it.

Many of the Nova Scotia coal mines have been in the hands of small companies who have been doing business in a small way and have been afraid of competition of any kind. Things have now taken a different shape. The Whitney Company, organized by the Fielding Government, is a large concern, chiefly Amcrican, but including also some leading Canadians. Ample capital, improved machinery and generally better business methods will give the Nova Scotia coal trade a fair chance. Instead of being afraid of American competition this company has challenged it and would accept reciprocity in coal as a great boon, although the other companies have been for some years declaiming against it. This big company has been formed with the full knowledge that the coal question is a much debated one and that at no distant day coal must be made free. Knowing this well the company have subscribed their capital and gone on with their business. The abolition of the coal duty might create some disturbance of trade arrangements at the beginning. But there is little reason to doubt that in a short time the business would get down to a solid basis and would prosper in common with other industries. One great advantage of the Liberal policy to the coal trade is that by a reduction of the tariff, many articles required by the companies for the development of mining operations would be made cheaper, and the workmen would benefit by the cheapening of food, clothing and other things.

## Has the N. P. Given Employment to the People ?

Tory speakers point with enultation to the census returns as proving affirmatively this question. If an enquirer is not satisfied on this point by the exodus during the decade '81 to '91, let him return to rhe same census returns and analize them.

The Statistical Abstract for 1881, page 180, which purports to give this analysis, states that there are in Canada 1,659,355 persons whose occupations are given by the census. They are divided into classes as follows:

| | |
|---|---:|
| Agriculture | 735,201 |
| Fishing | 27,079 |
| Lumbering | 11,756 |
| Mining | 15,168 |
| Total, | 790,210 |

| | |
|---|---:|
| Trade and Transportation (including sailors 14,000, railway employees 23,000, expressmen and teamsters 17,000, retail traders 40,000, etc | 186,595 |
| Manufacturing and Mechanical pursuits | 320,001 |
| Domestic and Personal Service | 246,113 |
| Professional Avocations | 63,210 |
| Non-productive Class | 52,986 |
| Total, | 1,659,355 |

How many of these classes are benefitted by the National Policy?

It is contended that those engaged in **manufacturing and mechanical pursuits, 320,000** are largely dependant on this National Policy, but it must be remembered that a very great many of these industries that give employment were flourishing industries under the revenue tariff which prevailed up to 1878. It would therefore be a gross mistake to conclude that the 310,000 persons engaged in manufacturing and mechanical pursuits are in any way dependant upon the existence of a high tariff. On the contrary, it will be found that a very small proportion of them are so dependant.

The same Statistical Abstract gives the most numerous of the various employments of these 320,000 as follows, and it is submitted these are not directly benefitted by the National Policy, but indirectly and largely injured.

| | |
|---|---|
| Carpenters and Joiners, | 45,769 |
| Dressmakers, Milliners and Seamstresses, | 36,494 |
| Blacksmiths, | 18,545 |
| Boot and Shoemakers, | 16,119 |
| Tailors and Tailoresses, | 15,094 |
| Saw and Planing Mill Operators, | 13,338 |
| Masons, | 10,312 |
| Painters and Glaziers | 10,202 |
| Machinists, | 9,572 |
| Butchers, | 7,238 |
| Compositors and Pressmen, | 6,550 |
| Ship and Boatbuilders, | 4,435 |
| Turners, | 4,975 |
| Millers, | 4,384 |
| Moulders, | 4,070 |
| Curriers and Tanners, | 3,713 |
| Harness and Saddlery, | 3,647 |
| Bakers, | 4,551 |
| Brickmakers, | 3,138 |
| Cheese Factories and Creameries, | 3,438 |
| Coopers, | 3,204 |
| Marble and Stone Cutters, | 3,585 |
| Plasterers, | 2,500 |
| Plumbers, | 3,249 |
| Lumbermen, | 12,319 |
| Tinsmiths, | 4,740 |
| | |
| | 255,181 |

A careful examination of the census shows that out of the above number of 320,000 persons, there is a very small propor. tion who may reasonably be supposed to be benefitted by the National Policy. The following table shows the chief ones :

Mill operatives (cotton) by vol. 2 of census
returns 6,053; by vol 3.................................6,953
Mill operatives (woollen) by vol 2—4,421;
by vol 3.............................................6,139
Mill operatives (textile and not specified).........3,876
Manufacturers and officials of Manufacturing
Companies............................................6,169
Mineral and Soda Water Makers, (by vol. 2,
354, and by 3rd vol.....................................  643
Glass Blowers and Workers, (by 2 vol. 581,
and by 3rd vol..........................................  689
Hat and Cap Makers,.....................................  368
Hosiery and Knitting Mill operatives (by 2nd
vol. 946, and by 3rd vol............................1,803
Linen Mill operatives, (by 2nd vol. 48, and
by 3rd vol.............................................    1
Oil Works employes (by vol. 2—167, and
by 3rd volume...........................................  276
Organ Makers...........................................  368
Rope, Twine and Cordage factory operatives...  627
Sugar Makers and Refiners...........................1,927
Umbrella and Parasols..................................   97
Silk Mill operatives...................................  294

                                                      ——————
                                                      30,239

These 30,000 represent the proportion of the 320,000 engaged in those industries which may fairly be said to in any way owe their existence or continuance in operation to the Protective tariff.

It may be said that the mining interest is protected and encouraged, and there is no doubt that this is so. The statistics show that there is engaged in Canada :

Agriculture.................................................735,207
Fishing........................................................ 27,079
Lumbering..................................................... 12,756
Mining and Quarrying............................... 15,168

                                              ——————
                          Total,.......... 790,210

These 15,000 may be benefitted, but it is at the expense of the other 775,000.

In the Maritime Provinces the total number engaged in mining is :

| | | |
|---|---|---|
| In Nova Scotia | - - - - - | 5,660 |
| In New Brunswick, | - - - - - | 97 |
| In P. E. Island, | - - - - - - | 18 |
| | Total, | 5,775 |

As no P.E. Island resident has ever discovered these eighteen or know where they "mine," some doubt may be cast upon these figures.

Of the 700,000 farmers and their sons engaged in farming in Canada, the census show that in Old Canada, that is New Brunswick, Nova Scotia, P. E. Island, Ontario and Quebec, during the ten years, 1881 to 1891, there was a decrease of 36,000, in the Maritime Provinces—

| | | | | |
|---|---|---|---|---|
| New Brunswick lost | - | - | - | 8,605 Farmers |
| Nova Scotia | " - | - | - | 10,095 " |
| P. E. Island | " | - | - | 265 " |

Total decrease of farmers for Maritime Provinces 18,965

## Do Duties on Agricultural Products Protect the Farmers ?

But the Tory orator contends the N. P., by the imposition of duties upon **Animals, Meats, Eggs. Butter Cheese, Apples, Beans, Hay, Barley, Oats. Oatmeal, &c.,** largely benefits the farmer.

As to most of these articles but little is said, as we are well known to be large **Exporters** and not **Importers** of them, and the argument that the imposition of duties on articles we don't import protects the farmer or gives him a higher price is felt to be absurd.

For instance, no reasonable man could successfully contend that oats, barley, eggs, potatoes, hay, etc., of which we are enormous exporters, are enhanced in price to the farmer, or that mackerel, etc., could be enhanced in price to the fisherman by any duty that could be put on. One hundred per cent. would have the same effect as ten per cent., and neither would have any effect, as we do not import, but export.

But it is said this reply will not cover the case of hogs, pork, or beef. Let us see if this is so.

The following table taken from the Trade and Navigation Returns for 1894 shews the quantity and value of **imports of animal products** for home consumption, with the quantity and value exported in 1893.

| | Imports for home consumption. | | Exports of Canadian Produce. | |
|---|---|---|---|---|
| | Value. | No. of lbs. | Value. | No. of lbs. |
| Butter, | $ 46,637 | 224,384 | $ 1,296.814 | 7,036.013 |
| Cheese. | 20,964 | 116,106 | 13,407,470 | 133,946,365 |
| Lard (rendered) | 12,620 | 146,885 | 66,773 | 709,624 |
| Meats, viz: | | | | |
| Bacon & Hams, Sh'lders & Sides } | 76.088 | 670,155 | 1,970,318 | 18,504,347 |
| Beef salt'd in brls· | 95.575 | 2,316,588 | 21,279 | 356,106 |
| Mutton, | 149 | 2,132 | 7,671 | 89,957 |
| Pork (barrelled) | 272.000 | 3,862,546 | 81,953 | 903,022 |
| Poultry & Game, | 12,297 | . . . . . . | 20,840 | . . . . . . |
| Canned Meats. . . . . . . . . | | . . . . . . | 1,005,087 | 10,115,626 |
| Other meats, fresh and salted, | 38,799 | 426,990 | 24,991 | 418,598 |
| Total. . . . . | $575,129 | 7,765,786 lbs. | $ 17,903,396 | 172,079.658 |

**Of Agricultural Produce we export and import as follows:**

| | EXPORTS. No of Bushels. | Imports for home consumption. No. of Bushels. |
|---|---|---|
| Barley, | 2,040,648 | 2,138 |
| Beans, | 276,313 | 13,752 |
| Buckwheat, | 594,604 | 10 |
| Oats, | 7,273,906 | 44,264 |
| Peas (whole) | 3,255,810 | } 11,032 |
| Peas (split) | 158,536 | |
| Rye, | 59,121 | ,302 |
| Wheat, | 9,271,855 | 9,069 |
| Other Grain, | 39,958 | . . . . . . |
| Total bushels, | 22.970,781 | 80.567 |
| " value, | $ 13,831,969 | ,$ 167,500 |

## Potatoes and Hay.

Of potatoes Canada exports 1,112,830 bushels of a value of $422,000 and imports for home consumption, only 37,571 bushels of the value of $8000.

Of hay she exports 151,851 tons of a value of $1,452,872 and imports for home consumption 1494 tons of a value of $14,000.

## Mackerel.

Of mackerel Canada exports in fresh, canned and pickled 536,453 dollars worth and imports in fresh and pickled only 1858 dollars worth.

These tables conclusively show that with respect to all these Agricultural products and fish Canada is a **great exporting country**—and the imposition of duties on these articles with the idea of protecting the farmer or fisherman is a blind and a humbug.

The price the farmer or fisherman receives is governed by the markets of the world to which we export. The British market fixes the price of our wheat, oats and peas, bacon and ham, cheese and butter. The American market fixes the price of our barley, beans, mackerel, wood, hay, potatoes, eggs, horses, sheep, poultry, hides, pelts.

All the duties in the world imposed by us on these articles. cannot in any way affect the price, because we don't import them but export.

A frantic effort is being made to induce the farmer to believe that pork and beef are exceptions to this rule and that the duties are a protection to the farmer and keep out American pork and beef. There is nothing whatever in this argument.

While we import a much larger quantity of barrelled pork than we export, we at the same time export nearly $2,000,000 worth of bacon and ham, and import of them practically nothing ($76,000). Our ham and bacon exports are therefore twenty-five times as much as our imports and our total pork exportation including hams, bacon, etc., besides barrelled pork is about six times the value of the importation for home consumption.

The barrelled pork we import is used chiefly by the lumbermen and does not enter into competition with such pork as P. E. Island produces.

As a fact barrelled pork is often cheaper in Chicago than in Toronto (the two great pork centres for U. S. and Canada) while at the same time the farmer is getting more for his live hog in Chicago than in Toronto.

The explanation of this seeming anomaly lies in the fact that the Chicago packer utilizes the hog in packing better than we do.

Everything including the blood, bristles and even the offal is utilized and turned into something of money value, and the Chicago man gets a higher price for the hams and belly bacon not put in the barrel.

If the duty was taken off pork to-morrow it would not increase the price paid to the farmer in Canada for his hog in the slightest.

The buyer and pork packer in P. E. Island regulates the price he pays the farmer by the prices ruling in Chicago.

If these prices go up he raises, if they go down he lowers. The duty does not enter into his calculations at all, nor does the Chicago pork come into serious competition with him.

The lumberman will buy the Chicago pork, and pay the duty. It is preferred by the shanty man.

Canadian pork is used for home consumption and is preferred to the American pork.

## Reform of the Tariff!

Many people were led to believe from the statements made by Ministers, and from the fact that they spent a year going over Canada pretending to ascertain the workings of the National Policy among the people, that it was their intention to reform the the tariff. A great flourish of trumpets was made on this point, and a new tariff was actually introduced by Mr. Foster at the session of '94. His original resolutions proposed several hundreds of changes, all in the direction of lightening the burdens of the people Among other things, specific duties as such were to be abolished, but as time progressed and the different manufacturers were able to bring their influence to bear, the proposed changes and reductions were abandoned. Specific duties were restored, and with the exception of a reduction made on agricultural implements and binder twine, the tariff remains substantially as onerous as before. This can be proved beyond any doubt by taking the monthly returns published in the Canada Gazette, showing the quantity and value of goods entered for consumption and the duty collected thereon in each month.

Take the month of December, 1894. The total value of dutiable goods entered was $4,262,352 ; the duty paid was $1,347,603, or about 31½ per cent.

The average of the present tariff, therefore, is as nearly as possible the same as the old tariff.

By the last Trade and Navigation Returns, 1894, we are enabled to show what the taxes exacted on each class of goods were.

The following is a list:

| | VALUE. | DUTY PAID. | PER CENT. |
|---|---|---|---|
| Carriages, - - - | $ 408,787 | $ 127.891 | 31.3 |
| Manufactures of Cotton, - | 4,557,492 | 1,295,843 | 28.4 |
| Earthenware and China, | 709,737 | 238,429 | 33.6 |
| Manufac. of Flax, Hemp and Jute, | 1,618,983 | 360.951 | 22.3 |
| Fruits (dry and green) - | 1,817,450 | 461,000 | 25.3 |
| Manufactures of Glass, - | 1,219,543 | · 324,566 | 26.6 |
| Hats, Caps, etc., - - | 1,320,000 | 396,191 | 30.0 |
| Manufactures of Iron and Steel, | 10,113,177 | 2,878,368 | 28.4 |
| Musical Instruments, - | 375,421 | 103,110 | 27.5 |
| Oils of all kinds, Mineral, Animal, Vegetable, etc., - - | 1,297,421 | 681,256 | 52.5 |
| Paper and manufactures of, including Wall Paper, etc., - | 1,187.236 | 401,715 | 33.8 |
| Provisions, - - | 734,481 | 204,311 | 27.8 |
| Soaps, - - - | 176,959 | 64,580 | 36.6 |
| Champagne and Sparkling Wines, | 166,785 | 91,311 | 54.8 |
| (N.B.—WINES.—Compare with Kerosene Oil, which pays about 160 per cent.) | | | |
| Vegetables (melons, potatoes, tomatoes, fresh corn and baked beans in cans, - - - | 220.631 | 53,408 | 24.2 |
| Wood and manufactures of, - | 1,087,128 | 298,564 | 27.4 |
| Wool and manufactures of (blankets, cloths, tweeds, flannels, socks, shawls, cloaks, shirts, carpets, etc.) - - | 10,946,244 | 3,309.389 | 30.2 |
| Total dutiable goods, - | $69,873,571 | $21,161,710 | 30.8 |

## Specific Duties.

Among the many promises of the tariff revision (in 1894) was the total or partial abolition of specific duties. These duties, levied on the pound, the yard, the bushel, or the dozen, are unfairly heavy on consumers of cheaper grades of goods. To tax a yard of cheap cloth the same amount as a yard of superior quality is a manifest injustice to consumers of coarser lines. This injustice pertains to all/ specific duties, and as in other objectional features of the Canadian tariff the revision has left matters little or no better than before. The injustice is in proportion to the fluctuation and range of prices. As an instance, the tax of two cents per lb. on raspberries, cherries, strawberries, etc., is trifling when such small fruit are expensive luxuries

But, when the price falls and they become articles of common use, it may be as high as fifty per cent. The Government has a two-fold object in retaining this class of duties. They lessen the burden on wealthy consumers, who are able most effectually to oppose the protective system, and they keep the public in ignorance of the extent to which they are taxed. An innocent-looking tax of a few cents per pound or per yard may, and does, conceal duties of more than 100 per cent. The following list shows some of the unjust discriminations effected by specific duties in the new Canadian tariff. It does not contain all the discriminations, and the widest variations have not been presented :

| | Rate of Duty. | Upon an assumed cost of | Rate per cent. of duty. |
|---|---|---|---|
| Collars, per doz.... | 24c per doz. and 25 p. ct. | $0.72 | 58 1-3 |
| " " .... | " " " | 1.44 | 41 2-3 |
| Cuffs " pairs.. | 4c. per pair and 25 p. c. | 96 | 75 |
| " " ...... | " " " | 1.92 | 50 |
| Shirts " ...... | $1 per doz. and 25 p. c. | 4.00 | 50 |
| " " ...... | " " " | 20.00 | 30 |
| Blankets, per lb..... | 5c. per lb. and 25 p. c. | 40 | 37½ |
| " " ...... | " " " | 65 | 33 |
| Oilcloth per yard... | ⎱ 30 p. c. but not less than | 8 | 50 |
| " " ... | ⎰ 4c. per square yard. | 75 | 30 |
| Wall paper, borders per roll | ⎱ 1½c per roll and | 9 | 41 2-3 |
| " " | ⎰ 25 per cent. | 75 | 27 |
| Tweeds, per yard | ..... ............. | 25 | 65 |
| " " | ..................... | 2.00 | 30 |
| Coatings " | ..................... | 1.00 | 35 |
| " " | ..................... | 6.00 | 26 2-3 |
| Overcoatings, " | ............. ....y.... | 50 | 65 |
| " " | ..................... | 7.00 | 28 |
| Castile soap, per lb..... | 2c. per lb.......... | 12 | 16 2-3 |
| " " .... | " .......... | 20 | 10 |
| Canned fish " | .... 1½c. per can or p'kge. | 10 | 15 |
| " " | ..................... | 20 | 7½ |
| | (This duty is levied on the can) | | |
| Books........ | 6c. per lb.......... | cheap | 100 |
| " ........ | " .......... | dear | 1 |
| Soap, common, per lb.. | 1c per lb.......... | 5 | 20 |
| " " " | ..................... | 10 | 10 |
| Clothes wringers, each.. | 25c. each and 20 p. c. | 4.00 | 26¼ |
| " " .. | " " | 10.00 | 22½ |
| Ready-made clothing, per suit.............. | | 8.00 | 42 |
| " " " | .............. | 30.00 | 33 |

| Rate of Duty. | Upon an assumed cost of | Rate per cent. of duty. |
|---|---|---|
| Socks and stockings per doz. pair ⎱ 10c per doz. | 60 | 51 2-3 |
| "        "        "        ⎰ and 35 p.c. | 10.00 | 36 |
| Dessicated Cocoa, per lb...5c per lb | 12 | 41 2-3 |
| "        "        ..        " | 15 | 33 1-3 |
| Rice, per lb...........1¼c. per lb | 5 | 25 |
| "    "    ...............    " | 10 | 12 1-2 |
| Raisins, per lb..........1c. per lb | 5 | 20 |
| "    "    .........    " | 12 1-2 | 8 |
| Prunes, "    .........1c. per lb | 4 | 25 |
| "    "    .........    " | 15 | 6 2-3 |
| Currants, dried, per lb...1c. per lb | 6 | 16 2-3 |
| "        "    ...    " | 10 | 10 |
| Vinegar, per gal.......15c. per gal | 15 | 100 |
| "    ,"    .......    " | 30 | 50 |
| Corn Starch, farina,etc.1½c. per lb | 10 | 15 |
| "        "    | 18 | 8 1-3 |
| Coal Oil...............6c. per gal | | from 60 to 100 |
| Carpets, cotton warp,per yard,3c. per yard and 25 p. c. | 20 | 40 |
| "        "        "    | 50 | 31 |
| "    all wool    " 5c per sq. yd. and 25 p. c. | 50 | 35 |
| "        "        "        "        " | 1.00 | 30 |
| Cordage, per lb.......1¼c. per lb and 10 p. c. | 10 | 22 1-2 |
| "        "    .....    "        "    "    " | 20 | 16 1-4 |
| Window shades, per yd ⎱ 35 p. c. but not less | 10 | 50 |
| "        "    ⎰ 5c. per sq. yard, | 20 | 35 |
| Baking Powder per lb....6c. per lb | 30 | 20 |
| "        "    ...    " | 60 | 10 |

On tweeds, etc., where the duty is not stated above, the tariff taxes the goods per pound weight, thus manifestly pressing more heavily upon the coarser and heavier goods.

### Extracts From the Tariff.

The following are the duties imposed by the tariff upon some of the articles in common use :

Adzes and hatchets ............ 35 per cent.

Agate iron-ware, .............. 35 "

Agricultural implements : Mowing machines, self-binding harvesters, harvesters without binders binding attachments, reapers, sulky and walking ploughs, harrows, cultivators, seed drills and horse rakes, ............ 20 "

Agricultural implements: Axes of all kinds, scythes hay knives, lawn mowers, pronged forks, rakes, hoes and other agricultural tools or implements, 35 "

Agricultural implements : Shovels, spades, 50 cts.
   per dozen and                                             25 per cent.
Axle grease,              .............   25    "
Bags or sacks of hemp, linen or jute, and cotton
   seamless bags,          ............   20    "
Bags, cotton, made by the needle,     ........   32½   "
Bags, paper, printed or plain,       ............   25    "
Baking powder,            ............   6c. per lb.
Barbed wire fencing of iron or steel,    ............   ¾c.  "
Binder twine,              ...............   12½ per cent.
Blankets             5c. per lb. and   25   "
Blueing, (laundry)         ............   25    "
Bolts, nuts and washers(iron or steel)1c. per lb and   20   "
Bolts, nuts and washers (iron or steel, less than 3-8
   inch in diameter)1c. per lb, and 25 per cent.,
   but not less than                   35    "
Boots and shoes (leather)      .............   25    "
Braces or suspenders.        .............   35    "
Braids,                  ............   30    "
Brass nails, rivets, screws, etc.,     ............   30    "
Brushes,               .............   25    "
Buckles, iron or steel,        ............   27½   "
   "   brass,          •      ............   30    "
Builders' hardware,         .............   32½   "
Buttons, pantaloons, etc.,      ............   20    "
Candles, paraffine wax,       ............   4c. per lb.
   "  (other than above);    ............   25 per cent:
Candy and confectionery,      ............   35    "
Caps and hats, fur,         ............   25    "
Caps and hats and bonnets,      ............   30    "
Carpenters' rules,         .............   35    "

Carpets (two-ply and three-ply ingrain, whose warp
   is wholly composed of cotton or other material
   than wool worsted, hair of alapaca goat or
   like animals),     ......... 3c. per square yard and   25   "
Carpets (treble ingrain, three-ply or two-ply composed wholly of wool) 5c. per square yard and   25   "
Carpets (other than above)      .............   30    "
Carriages, buggies. pleasure carts and similar
   vehicles (not elsewhere specified). Costing not
   more than $50, $5 each and 25 per cent; costing
   more than $50                    35    "
Carriages : Farm and freight wagons, carts drays
   and similar vehicles ....................................   25    "

| | | |
|---|---|---|
| Chains, trace, tug and halter | 32½ | per cent |
| Chimneys, lamp, glass, | 30 | " |
| China ware and porcelain ware | 30 | " |
| Churns, wood | 20 | " |
| Crocks and churns, earthenware, 3c. per gallon of holding capacity | | |
| Clothes wringers ............25c. each and | 20 | " |
| Cordage ........1¼c. per lb. and 10 p. c. | 2⅛c per lb. | |
| Collars, cotton, linen, etc............24c. per doz. and | 25 per cent. | |
| Cuffs " " ........4c. per pair and | 25 | " |
| Cultivators | 20 | " |
| Currycombs and currycards | 32½ | " |
| Cutlery, table, not plated | 32½ | " |
| " " plated | 35 | " |
| " N. O. P., not plated | 25 | " |
| Cutters and sleighs | 30 | " |
| Duke, cotton, printed, dyed or colored | 30 | " |
| Earthenware and stoveware, jugs, crocks, etc. 3c. per gallon capacity | | |
| Earthenware, viz., drain pipe and tiles | 35 | " |
| " drain tiles not glazed | 20 | " |
| Edged tools; n. e. s | 35 | " |
| Envelopes, printed or not | 3 0 | " |
| FLOUR, | 75c. per bbl. | |
| Fanning mills and parts, | 35 per cent. | |
| Barbed wire fencing of iron or steel | ¾c. per lb. | |
| Buckthorn and strip fencing of iron or steel | ½c. " | |
| Fertilizers, compounded or manufactured | 10 per cent. | |
| Flags, bunting or cotton, | 30 | " |
| Forks, pronged, hay, manure, etc., | 35 | " |
| Furniture, all kinds, | 30 | " |
| Glass Goods, lamp chimneys, etc., | 30 | " |
| Mirrors, | 27½ to 32½ | " |
| Axle grease, | 25 | " |
| Grindstones, | 30 | " |
| Halter chains, | 32½ | " |
| Hammers, | 25 | " |
| Harrows and parts, | 20 | " |
| Hats, caps and bonnets, not fur, | 30 | " |
| Hay knives, | 35 | " |
| Hay rakes, wood, | 35 | " |
| India rubber and waterproof clothing, | 35 | " |
| Linen clothing, | 32½ | " |
| Mangles, washing, | 27½ | " |
| Harvest mitts and mitts and gloves of all kinds | 35 | " |

| | | |
|---|---|---|
| Nails and spikes, | ............ | 30 per cent. |
| Wire nails, | ............ | 1c. per lb. |
| Cut nails, | ............ | ¾c. per lb. |
| COAL OIL (equal to from 100 to 150 per cent) | | 6c. per gal. |
| Ploughs, walking and sulky, | ............ | 20 per cent. |
| Horse rakes, | ............ | 20 " |
| Rakes, not elsewhere specified, | ............ | 35 " |
| Rice, cleaned, | ............ | 1¼c. per lb. |
| Saws of all kinds, | ............ | 32½ per cent. |
| Screw nails, | ............ | 35 " |
| Scythes, | ............ | 35 " |
| Scythe stones, | ............ | 30 " |
| Separators and parts, | ............ | 30 " |
| Shears (pruning and sheep) | ............ | 35 " |
| Sleighs and sledges, | ............ | 30 " |
| Soap (common) | ............ | 1c. per lb. |
| Soap (castile, mottled or white) | ............ | 2c. " |
| Starch, | ............ | 1½c. " |
| Steam engines, (portable) | ............ | 30 per cent. |
| Stoves, | ............ | 27½ " |
| Stove pipes, | ............ | 27½ " |
| Stove shovels, | ............ | 27½ " |
| Sugar (raw above 16 Dutch standard and all refined) | ......... | 64c. per 100 lbs. |
| Syrup, | ............ | ¾c. per lb. |
| Molasses, | ............ | 1½c. per lb. |
| Surcingles (cotton or hemp) | ............ | 30 per cent: |
| Suspenders and braces, | ............ | 35 " |
| Underwear of all kinds, | .......30 to 35 " |
| Washing machines, | ............ | 27½ " |
| Winceys, checked, striped or fancy cotton | ............ | 30 " |
| Windmills, | ............ | 30 " |

" The customs tariff of the Dominion should be based, not as it is now, upon the protective Principle, but upon the requirements of the public service ; and it should be so adjusted as to make free, or to bear as lightly as possible upon the necessaries of life, and should be so arranged as to promote free trade with the whole world, more particularly with Great Britain and the United States."

# ENLARGED MARKETS—RECIPROCITY.

## Plank 2—Liberal Platform.

" That, having regard to the prosperity of Canada and the United States as adjoining countries, with many mutual interests, it is desirable that there should be the most friendly relations and broad and liberal trade intercourse between them ;

" That the interests alike of the Dominion and of the Empire would be materially advanced by the establishing of such relations ;

" That the period of the old receprocity treaty was one of marked prosperity to the British North American colonies;

" That the pretext under which the Government appealed to the country in 1891 respecting negotiation for a treaty with the United States was misleading and dishonest, and intended to deceive the electorate;

" That no sincere effort has been made by them to obtain a treaty but that, on the contrary, it is manifest that the present Government, controlled as they are by monopolies and combines, are not desirous of securing such a treaty;

" That the first step towards obtaining the end in view, is to place a party in power who are sincerely desirous of of promoting a teaty on terms honorable to both countries;

" That a fair and liberal reciprocity treaty would develop the great natural resources of Canada, would enormously increase the trade and commerce between the two countries,would tend to encourage friendly relations between the two peoples, would remove many causes which have in the past provoked irritation and trouble to the Governments of both countries, and would promote those kindly relations between the Empire and the Republic which afford the best guarantee for peace and prosperity;

" That the Liberal party is prepared to enter into negotiations with a view to obtaining such a treaty, including a well-considered list of manufactured articles, and we are satisfied that any treaty so arranged will receive the assent of Her Majesty's Government, without whose approval no treaty can be made.

---

### The Benefits of Reciprocity.

Reciprocity is not a mere theory as regards the effects to be produced. The old reciprocity treaty extending from 1854 to 1866 affords practical illustration of the benefits to be derived from interchange of trade with the United States. During the twelve years that treaty remained in operation our exports to the United States nearly quadrupled, rising from $10,473,000 in 1854 to $39,950,000 in 1866 from all the provinces now embraced within the bounds 'of the Dominion. The period during which the treaty remained in force was one of marked prosperity for all the provinces  Since the abrogation of the treaty in 1866 our export trade with the United States has practically remained stationary, though maintaining the average annual increase from 1854 to 1866 would have carried it up for 1893 to over $100,000.000, the actual amount having been for that year $37,296,110 of the produce of Canada, not including coin and bullicn, the produce of Canada, which amounted to an additional $309,459.

## Sham Negotiations,

It is obvious that the advantages to be derived from reciprocity are very great, and it is to be regretted that the Government has been guilty of duplicity in dealing with the question. When Parliament was dissolved in February, 1891, the reason assigned for the act was that a treaty of reciprocity with the United States was about to be made, and that it would be desirable to refer the treaty to a Parliament fresh from the people, and not to a moribund House Statements in Government organs that a reciprocity treaty in natural products similar to the treaty of 1854 was being negotiated at Washington, and that Sir Charles Tupper was going there as Canadian Commissioner, attracted attention in the United States, and on January 29th, 1891, Congressman Baker addressed a letter to Mr. Blaine, Secretary of State, asking if these rumors were well founded. To this enquiry Mr. Blaine made the following unequivocal reply :

WASHINGTON, D. C., 29th January, 1891.

MY DEAR MR. BAKER,—I authorize you to contradict the rumors you refer to. There are no negotiations whatever on foot for a reciprocity treaty with Canada, and you may be assured that no scheme for reciprocity with the Dominion confined to natural products will be entertained by this Government. I know nothing of Sir Charles Tupper's coming to Washington.

Yours very truly,

JAMES G. BLAINE

Five days after this letter had emphatically given the lie to the claim that reciprocity negotiations were in progress, Parliament was dissolved on the pretext above named. And the false representations thus made to the electors no doubt aided powerfully in securing a verdict favorable to the Government.

Having won the election upon these representations it became necessary to fulfill the promise to send commissioners to Washington, and this was done in April, 1891. Owing to indignation at the duplicity and misrepresentation of the Canadian authorities as to the action of the United States Government in the premises, President Harrison refused the Canadian commissioners an interview.

In February, 1892, Canadian commissioners succeeded through through the intervention of Sir Julien Pauncefortc in obtaining a reception by Hon James G. Blaine, American Secretary of State, and then stated their proposal for reciprocity to be on the basis of the treaty of 1854 and to be confined to natural products. To this proposal Mr. Blaine made answer that the United States would consider no proposition for reciprocity which did not embrace an agreed list of manufactures, as was well known to the Canadian commissioners from all previous declarations of the American State Department. In truth the Canadian proposals were a mockery made solely to save appearances.

The report made by Mr. Blaine to the President of his interview with the Canadian Commissioners in a state document, signed by him and published in the offcial records of Congress, contains the following:

"At the first conference, on February 10, the commissioners "stated that they were authorized by the Canadian Government to "propose the renewal of the reciprocity treaty of 1854 (which was "terminated in 1866 by the action of the Congress of the United "States), with such modifications and extensions as the altered "circumstances of both countries and their respective interests "might seem to require.

"In answer to an inquiry, the commissioners stated that the "modifications or extensions contemplated in the schedules of "articles *should be confined to natural products* and should *not* "*embrace manufactured articles.*

"The commissioners were informed that the Government of "of the United States would not be prepared to renew the treaty "of 1854 nor to agree upon any commercial reciprocity which "should be confined to natural products alone; and that in view of "the great development of industrial interests of the United States "and of the changed conditions of the commercial relations of the "two countries since the treaty of 1854 was negotiated, it was re-"garded of essential importance that *a list of manufactured goods* "*should be included* in the schedules of articles for free or favored "exchange in any reciprocity arrangement which might be made.

"The commissioners then inquired if the Government of the "United States would expect to have preferential treatment ex-"tended to the list of manufactured goods of the United States on "their introduction into Canada by virtue of a reciprocity treaty, "or whether it would regard the Canadian Government as at "liberty to extend the same favors to the manufactured goods of "other countries not parties to the treaty on their introduction "into Canada.

"The reply given them was that it was the desire of the Gov-"ernment of the United States to make a reciprocity convention "which would be exclusive in its application to the United States "and Canada, and that other countries which are not parties to it "should not enjoy gratuitously the favors which the two neighbor-

" ing countries might reciprocally concede to each other for valuable
" considerations and at a large sacrifice to their respective
" revenues.

" Upon receiving this reply, the Canadian commissioners
" asked that the further consideration of the subject be adjourned
" till another conference, to enable them to consult as to the course
" which they would adopt in view of the foregoing declaration."

" In the conference of the 11th the Canadian commissioners
" stated that they *had given careful consideration to the suggestion*
" *that manufactured goods should be included in the schedules of*
" *articles for exchange* in a reciprocity convention, and to the desire
" expressed by the Government of the United States that such
" American goods on their introduction into Canada should be
" accorded preferential treatment ever similar goods from other
" countries; and they announced, with an expression of regret, that
" they did not consider it possible to meet the expectations of the
" Government of the United States in these respects. In the first
" place they encountered a serious obstacle in the matter of
" revenue. If any considerable list of manufactured goods of the
" United States should be admitted free into Canada, it would
" entail a material loss to the Dominion treasury, and if the same
" favors were likewise extended to the merchandise of other
" countries the loss of revenue would be much greater. They felt
" that they would not be able to recoup these losses by other
" methods of taxation. In the second place, it seemed to be
" impossible for the Canadian Government, in view of its present
" political relations and obligations, to extend to American goods a
" preferential treatment over those of other countries. As Canada
" was a part of the British Empire, they did not consider it
" competent for the Dominion Government to enter into any com-
" mercial arrangement with the United States, from the benefits of
" which Great Britain and its colonies should be excluded.

" The announcement of these conclusions of the Canadian
" commissioners was accepted as a bar to further negotiations on
" this subject, and it was not again discussed except in connection
" with the fishing privileges on the Atlantic coast."

### FORMER RECIPROCITY TREATIES.

[Article III, Treaty with Great Britain of 1854.]

It is agreed that the articles enumerated in the schedule hereunto annexed,
being the growth and produce of the aforesaid British colonies or of the
United States, shall be admitted into each country respectively free of duty:

Grain, flour and breadstuff of all kinds.
Animals of all kinds.
Fresh, smoked and salted meats.
Cotton, wool, seeds and vegetables.
Undried fruits, dried fruits,
Fish of all kinds.
Products of fish, and of all other creatures living in the water.
Poultry, eggs.
Hides, furs, skins, or tails, undressed.
Stone, or marble, in its crude or unwrought state.
Slate.
Butter, cheese, tallow.
Lard, horns, manures,
Ores. of metals, of all kinds.
Coal.

Pitch, tar, turpentine, ashes.
Timber, and lumber of all kinds, round, hewed and sawed, unmanufactured in whole or in part.
Firewood
Plants, shrubs, and trees.
Pelts, wool.
Fish oil.
Rice, broom corn, and bark.
Gypsum, ground or unground.
Hewn, or wrought, or unwrought burr or grindstones.
Dyestuffs.
Flax, hemp, or tow, unmanufactured.
Unmanufactured tobacco.
Rags.

[Article IV, Dıaft of treaty with Great Britain, 1874.—Geo. Brown Treaty.]

It is agreed that the articles enumerated in Schedules A, B, and C, hereunto annexed, being the growth, produce or manufacture of the Dominion of Canada or of the United States, shall, on their importation from the one country into the other, from the 1st day of July, 1875, to the 30th day of June, 1876 (both included), pay only two thirds of the duties payable at the date of this treaty on the importations into such country of such articles respectively; and from the 1st day of July, 1876, to the 30th day of June, 1877, (both included), shall pay one-third of such duties, and on and after the 1st day of July, 1877, for the period of years mentioned in article xiii of this treaty, shall be admitted free of duty into each country, respectively.

For the term mentioned in article xiii no other or higher duties shall be imposed in the United States upon other article not enumerated in said schedules the growth, produce or manufacture of Canada, or in Canada upon such other articles the growth, produce or manufacture of the United States, than are respectively imposed upon like articles the growth, produce or manufacture of Great Britain, or of any other country.

SCHEDULE A.

Consists of the following natural products:

Animals of all kinds.
Ashes, pot, pearl, and soda.
Bark.
Bark extract, for tanning purposes.
Bath bricks.
Breadstuffs of all kinds.
Bricks for building, and fire bricks.
Broom corn.
Burr or grindstones, hewed, wrought, or unwrought.
Butter,
Cheese.
Coal and coke.
Cotton wool.
Cotton waste.
Dyestuffs.
Earths, clays, ochers, sand, ground or unground.

Eggs.
Fish of all kinds.
Fish, products of, and of all other creatures living in the water, except fish preserved in oil.
Firewood.
Flax, unmanufactured.
Flour, and meals of all kinds.
Fruits, green or dried.
Furs, undressed.
Grain of all kinds.
Gypsum, ground, unground, or calcined.
Hay.
Hemp, unmanufactured.
Hides.
Horns.
Lard.
Lime.

Malt.
Manures.
Marble, stone, slate, or granite, wrought or unwrought.
Meats, fresh, smoked or salted.
Ores of all kinds of metals.
Pelts.
Pease, whole or split.
Petroleum oil,crude,refind or benzole.
Pitch.
Plants.
Poultry and birds of all kinds.
Rags of all kinds.
Rice.
Salt.
Seeds.

Shrubs.
Skins.
Straw,
Tails.
Tallow.
Tar.
Timber and lumber of all kinds,round, hewed and sawed, manufactured in whole or in part.
Tobacco, unmanufactured.
Tow, unmanufactured.
Trees.
Turpentine.
Vegetables.
Wool.

## SCHEDULE B.

Consisting of the following agricultural implements:

Axes.
Bagholders.
Beehives.
Bone-crushers, or parts thereof.
Cultivators, or parts thereof.
Chaff-cutters, or parts thereof.
Corn-huskers, or parts thereof.
Cheese-vats.
Cheese-factory heaters.
Cheese-presses, or parts thereof.
Churns, or parts thereof.
Cattle-feed boilers and steamers, or parts thereof.
Ditchers, or parts thereof.
Field rollers, or parts thereof.
Fanning mills, or parts thereof-
Feed-choppers or parts thereof.
Forks for hay and manure, hand or horse.
Grain Drills, or parts thereof.
Grain-crushers, or parts thereof.
Harrows.

Hoes, hand or horse.
Horserakes.
Horse-power machines,or parts thereof
Hay tedders, or parts thereof.
Liquid manure carts, or parts thereof.
Manure sowers, or parts thereof.
Mowers, or parts thereof.
Oil and oil-cake crushers, or parts thereof.
Plows, or parts thereof.
Root and seed planters, or parts thereof.
Root cutters, pulpers, and washers, or parts thereof.
Rakes.
Reapers, or parts thereof.
Reaper and mower combined, or parts thereof.
Spades.
Shovels.
Scythes.
Snaiths.
Threshing machines, or parts thereof.

## SCHEDULE C.

Consisting of the following manufactures, –

Axles, all kinds.
Boots and shoes, of leather.
Boot and shoe making machines.
Buffalo robes dressed and trimmed.
Cotton grain bags.
Cotton denims.
Cotton jeans, unbleached.
Cotton drillings, unbleached.
Cotton tickings.
Cotton plaids.
Cottonades. unbleached,
Cabinet ware and furniture, or parts thereof.

Carriages, carts, wagons. and other wheeled vehicles and sleighs or parts thereof.
Fire engines, or parts thereof.
Felt covering for boilers.
Gutta-percha belting and tubing.
Iron, bar, hoop, pig, puddled, rod, sheet, or scrap.
Iron nails, spikes, bolts, tacks brads or sprigs.
Iron castings.
India rubber belting and tubing.

Locomotives for railways, or parts thereof.

Lead, sheet or pig.

Leather sole or upper.

Leather, harness, and saddlery of

Mill, or factory, or steomboat fixed engines and machines or parts teereof

Manufactures of marble, stone, slate or granite.

Manufacturers of wood solely,or wood nailed, bound, hinged,or locked with metal materials.

Mangles, washing machines,wringing machines, and drying machines, or parts thereof.

Printing paper for newspapers.

Paper-making machines,or part tly reof.

Printing type, presses, and fo ers, paper cutters, ruling machines, age numbering machines and stere yp-ing apparatus, or parts thereof

Refrigerators, or parts thereof.

Railroad cars, carriages and trucks, or parts thereof.

Satinets of wood or cotton.

Steam engines or parts thereof.

Steel, wrought or cast, and steel plates and rails.

Tin tubes and piping.

Tweeds of wool solely.

Water-wheel machines and apparatus or parts thereof.

American duties have been imposed upon Canadian agricultural products imported into the United States since 186ᵣ. In October, 1890, these duties were largely increased by the McKi ᵤy Bill and the disastrous effect upon our export trade produced by this increase is shown by a comparison of farm exports for the year ending June 30th, 1890, the last year before the McKinley Bill went into operation, and the year ending June 30th, 1893, the last year for which we have full trade returns since the bil went into operation. The following is the comparison in twelve leading articles of farm products.

## Comparison of Export of Farm Products, 1890—1893.

| Name of Article, | 1890 | 1893 |
|---|---|---|
| Horses, | $1,887,895 | $1,123,339 |
| Cattle, | 104,623 | 11,032 |
| Poultry, | 105,612 | 52,114 |
| Eggs. | 1,793,104 | 324,355 |
| Wool, | 235,436 | 228,030 |
| Flax, | 175,563 | 124,082 |
| Barley, | 4,582,562 | 638,271 |
| Split peas, | 74,215 | 4,214 |
| Hay, | 922,797 | 854,958 |
| Malt, | 149,310 | 19 |
| Potatoes' | 308.915 | 259,176 |
| Rye, | 113,320 | 3,302 |
| | $10,453,352 | $3,624,892 |

## United States Market Compared With All Others.

It is the custom of the Conservative orators, and of the Con-servative press to seek to belittle the importance of the American market, and we are told that substitutes for that market can easily be obtained, as for instance in Australia, a country which last year took of the farm products of Canada to the value of $25 only. A statement of the lines in which our exports to the United States, even under the grievous restrictions of the McKinley Bill, exceeded our exports to all the rest of the world in 1893 will show how utterly destitute of foundation is this assertion. Here is the table which is more convincing than argument :

| Articles or classification of exports the produce of Canada. | United States. | All other countries. |
|---|---|---|
| Products of the mine, | $ 4,756,280 | $ 573,610 |
| " forest, | 13,859,960 | 12,49 ,950 |
| Fresh water fish and salt water fish, fresh, | 1,287,822 | 4,642 |
| Horses, | 1,123,339 | 337,818 |
| Swine, | 130,093 | 15,997 |
| Sheep, | 1,088,814 | 159,041 |
| Poultry, | 52,114 | 9,013 |
| Bones, | 58,444 | 10,282 |
| Hides, | 385,246 | 7,122 |
| Sheep pelts, | 66,939 | 16 |
| Wool, | 228,030 | 281 |
| Flax, | 124,082 | |
| Berries, | 96,104 | 115 |
| Fruit, N. E. S., | 24,646 | 1,114 |
| Barley, | 638,271 | 306,084 |
| Beans, | 351,058 | 4.624 |
| Hay, | 854,958 | 597,914 |
| Straw, | 25,117 | 932 |
| Maple sugar, | 48,174 | 1477 |
| Trees, shrubs and plants, | 11,959 | 232 |
| Potatoes, | 259,176 | 162,782 |
| Vegetables, | 105,836 | 10,404 |
| Other articles, | 27,096 | 1,577 |
| Fertilizers, | 7,706 | |
| Furs, | 6,664 | 3,103 |
| Grindstones, | 24,754 | 948 |
| Gypsum, | 27,091 | 2,356 |
| Household effects, | 1,246,085 | 37,081 |
| Lime, | 97,898 | 8.207 |
| Barrels, | 10,631 | 6.297 |
| Household furniture, | 123,872 | 50,749 |
| Wood pulp, | 424,253 | 1,640 |
| Other manufactures, | 249,752 | 117.727 |
| Bullion, | 309,459 | |
| | $28,132,233 | $14,932,145 |

# RECIPROCITY.

In connection with this subject of *Reciprocity* with the United States, the following tables are submitted showing the exports of the three Maritime Provinces, during 1893, and the countries where exported to:

### NEW BRUNSWICK.

Total exports, . . . . . . . . $ 7,253,611
Of these the United States took . . : , 3,735,074
 Over 50 per cent.
  The rest of the world took $ 3,518,537

Of this $3,518,537 Great Britain took almost $,3000,000, of which all but $225,000 was deal and deal ends.

Practically, therefore, New Brunswick's market for all she has to dispose of, except deals and deal ends, is found in the United States.

The products of her manufactures. $ 444,999
     " mines, 66,348
     " fisheries, 756,437
     " animals and their products, 158,041
     " agricultural produce, 174,763

All find their best markets in the United States, *while less than half a million* of her total exports find a market in all countries of the world outside of Great Britain and the United States.
The case is even stronger with

### PRINCE EDWARD ISLAND.

Her total exports in 1893 reached . . . $ 1,235,344
Of these the United States took . . . . 668.152
 or over 50 per cent
  All the rest of the world took $ 567,292

### NOVA SCOTIA.

Total exports, $10,308,628
Of these the United States took 3,230,218
 or nearly one third,
  All the rest of the world took $ 7,078.410

This is irrespective of $304,220 coin and bullion exported to the United States.

These tables show that one of the most *valuable markets* for the *Maritime Provinces* is the United States.

That it would be suicidal on our part not to cultivate and develop it,

That in spite of *hostile tariffs on both sides* our trade with the United States, in the years 1893-94 was as follows :

| | | |
|---|---|---|
| Nova Scotia, | exports to United States, | $ 3,230,218 |
| New Brunswick, | " " " | 3,735,074 |
| P. E. Island | " " " | 608,152 |

Total exports,          $ 7,573,444

| | | |
|---|---|---|
| Nova Scotia, | Imports from U S., | $ 2,465,575 |
| New Brunswick, | " " | 2,933,763 |
| P. E. Island | " " | 130,294 |

5,529,632

Total trade of Mar. Provinces with
with the United States in 1893-4.          $13,103,076

This trade is capable of infinite expansion. A reciprocity treaty would re-vivify trade, increase our exports and imports, duplicate our profits, increase the value of our lands, retain at home and give employment to our population.

We do not ignore the increasing value of our British trade. On the contrary we desire to increase it. That is evident by the resolution moved by Mr. Davies in Parliament, and voted down by the Tories :    Resolved that

" Inasmuch as Great Britain admits the products of Canada into her ports free of duty, this House is of the opinion that the present scale of duties exacted on goods mainly imported from Great Britain should be reduced."

We have and will have the British markets absolutely free. We want two strings to our bow. We want to make the American market as free as the revenue aequirements of both countries permit.

We know we could have negotiated a reasonable and fair Reciprocity treaty in 1891 or 1892, embracing a fair list of manufactured goods.

We believe such a treaty can yet be had. The task has been rendered exceedingly difficult by the blundering of the Tory Governments. But it is not insuperable ; and if a Liberal Government is returned to power we can reasonably hope for the successful negotiation of a Reciprocity treaty with the United States *at an early date.*

# PURITY OF ADMINISTRATION—CONDEMN CORRUPTION.

"That the convention deplores the gross corruption in the management and expenditure of public moneys which for years past has existed under the rule of the Conservative party, and the revelations of which by the different parliamentary committees of enquiry have brought disgrace upon the fair name of Canada.

"The Government which profited politically by these expenditures of public moneys whereof the people have been defrauded, and which, nevertheless, have never punished the guilty parties, must be held responsible for the wrong-doing. We arraign the Government for retaining in office a Minister of the Crown proved to have accepted very large contributions of money for election purposes from the funds of a railway company, which while paying the political contributions to him, a member of the Government, with one hand, was receiving Government subsidies with the other.

"The conduct of the minister and the approval of his colleagues after the proof became known to them are calculated to degrade Canada in the estimation of the world, and deserve the severe condemnation of the people."

## A Few Examples.

The force of the charge of corruption made against the Conservative Government, and the urgent condemnation they deserve can be best shown by a few examples.

The illustrations given are confined to cases involving the action of members of the present administration, or of their supporters in the House, who have been sustained in their wrong-doing by the ministry and the party in Parliament.

1. In the Caron case the evidence is complete of the levying by a Minister for a reptile fund of an enormous sum from those interested in railway government subsidies, and its expenditure by Ministers in electoral corruption. The exposure is more remarkable because the original charges were mutilated and enquiry largely stifled, on the motion of Mr. Bowell, the present First Minister.

2. The McGreevy Conspiracy illustrates the levying of corruption funds from contractors for public works, the complicity of Ministers, and the tampering with justice by the release of political criminals.

3. The Blind Share Case illustrates the encouragement and assistance given by Mr. Bowell, the new Premier, to the trafficking in Orders in Council.

4. The Cochrane Case is a gross case of the sale of public offices by a member of Parliament.

5. The Turcotte case is one where a Member of Parliament is maintained in his seat while drawing the profits from a Government contract.

## The Caron Case.

Sir Adolphe P. Caron, M. P., is the leader of the Conservative party in the Province of Quebec. and he ranks next to the Premier in the Cabinet, both in seniority of appointment and in influence.

In 1892, charges were made by Mr. J. D. Edgar, M. P., in the House of Commons that sums amounting to $100,000 and upwards were levied from Government contractors and those interested in certain railway subsidies, and were spent in the bribery of twenty-two constituencies in the District of Quebec, at the general election of 1887,

To investigate these charges, he demanded a reference to the Committee of Privileges and Elections. The members composing this committee are, in the proportion of two to one, supporters of the Government.

The Ministers did not dare to face a full enquiry, and therefore they put up Mr. Mackenzie Bowell, the present Premier, to move to strike out some, and to vary others of the charges.

The Tarte-McGreevy inquiry of the previous year was made before the Committee of Privileges and Elections, and it had been so damaging to the Government that they dared not again face the committee. Mr. Bowell, therefore, provided in his motion that the emasculated charges should be referred to a Royal Commission, to be appointed by the Government and selected by the accused. Mr. Bowell's motion was carried by the usual party majority.

Mr. Edgar very properly declined to appear at the sittings of this Royal Commission but sent to the Commissioners a list of his witnesses, whom they called and partially examined.

In due time the Royal Commission reported the evidence taken. The startling and disgraceful facts revealed before them, even under the limited scope of the inquiry, show that the Ministers had good reasons for dreading the more complete exposure that would have been made if the original charges had been gone into.

It was clearly shown that when Sir Adolphe Caron entered the Ministry in 1880, he was a shareholder of the construction company which received all the Government subsidies granted to the Quebec and Lake St. John Railway Company. After he entered the Government, the subsidies voted to that railway exceeded a million of dollars. The late Senator Ross was president of this company, and Mr. Beemer was the contractor, also deeply interested in the subsidies. Just before the elections of 1887, Sir Adolphe Caron applied for a political subscription from Senator Ross, who promptly gave him $25,000.

According to Mr. Beemer's books, there were also about the same time a number of other payments amounting to $25,000 more, which was charged to "A. P. C." and "G. E. F." These letters were sworn to have ment "A. P. Caron" and "General Election Fund." There can be no doubt that at least $50,000 were furnished towards a corruption fund in 1887, from those interested in the subsidies to this one railway. It was a great investment for them, of course, to make this contribution, for the Government have paid them $463,408 since 1887.

Then there was the Temiscouata Railway, which was also receiving Dominion subsidies, and was partially enquired into by the Royal Commissioners. They found in this instance, too, that $25,000 was set apart and expended by this railway for political purposes during the progress of the work of construction.

These sums went to swell a Reptile Fund for the District of Quebec alone, for the election of 1887, which amounted to $112,000 according to the figures of the McGreevy papers papers published in The Globe.

Out of the twenty-two counties where this fund was expended, the Government only carried ten seats, making an average cost to the country for each member returned to support them $11,200.

It is not at all unfair to assume that in the rest of the Dominion similar corruption funds have been provided by the same vile means for the elections of 1887, and for all elections.

The raising of these enormous sums before every general election is a well recognized practice of the Conservative party in Canada. Before another Royal Commission in 1873, it was proved that Sir Hugh Allen paid for the promise of the old Canadian Pacific Railway Charter, $365,000 to the election fund of the Conservative party in 1872. How much more they had from other sources for that election will never be known.

For each dollar that a contractor, or a subsidized railway company, or a tariff-protected monopolist, pays to reptile funds, he is in a position to demand a ten-fold return in the plunder of the public. By the acceptance of these bribes, the Government place themselves at the mercy of the contributors.

Since the exposures in the Caron case, several new Ministries have been constructed, and in each one of them Sir Adolphe Caron has been placed in a high and honorable position. His offence has been adopted by the Conservative party as their own, and he himself has boldly justified it in his place on the floor of Parliament in these memorable words: **"I say that under the same circumstances what I did on that occasion I would do again to-morrow in order to help my friends."**

## The McGreevy Conspiracy and the Langevin-Caron Reptile Fund.

In 1891, a number of charges were made in Parliament by Mr. Tarte, M. P., against Sir Hector Langevin, then Minister of Public Works, and Hon. T. McGreevy, M. P. Mr. Tarte alleged that the contracting firm of Larkin, Connolly & Co., were allowed by Sir Hector Langevin, then Minister of Public Works, with the assistance of Mr. McGreevy, to cheat the country out of hundreds of thousands of dollars on Government contracts.

These charges were referred to a Committee of the House for investigation, and the public were startled by the revelations of fraud and conspiracy by which the country was shown to have been robbed of about half a million of dollars. The full extent to which this money was applied to Tory Corruption Funds will never be known, but evidence was dragged out of unwilling witnesses that **$119,438** of it were paid for election expenses.

The famous Quebec District Election Fund of 1887 received **$20,000** from these contractors, and that fund was distributed for election purposes by two Ministers of the Crown, Sir Hector Langevin and Sir Adolphe P. Caron.

As an instance of the grossly corrupt uses that were made of this Reptile Fund, the case of Three Rivers, Sir Hector Langevin's own constituency, may be given. In 1887 the total number of votes cast for Sir Hector, the successful candidate, was 640. The sum returned by Sir Hector's agent and published as his total lawful election expenses was **$917.09.** The sum sent into the constituency from this fund alone was $13,150. No wonder he was successful after an expenditure of over $20 for every vote he received.

Messrs. McGreevy and Connolly were placed on trial for their part in this conspiracy to defraud, and on conviction in November, 1894, were sentenced to gaol for twelve months. How could a Conservative Government who owed their places to the support given them by these conspirators permit them to serve out their sentence? How could Sir Adolphe Caron, a noble knight and a Minister, who had received and expended in corruption, part of the proceeds of this conspiracy, allow his friends and pals to languish in prison while he was an adviser of the Crown? It was therefore represented to the Government that confinement did not agree with the prisoner's digestion, and they were liberated after but three months' imprisonment.

The eminent judge who tried the case (Mr. Justice Rose) said that the offence was only aggravated by the purposes of electoral corruption to which the proceeds of this conspiracy were applied ; yet it was the very baseness of the objects of the conspiracy that saved these culprits from the punishment of their crimes. To screen the criminal purveyors of the Reptile Fund the course of justice was tampered with and the prison doors were flung open wide for the escape of the men who had dark political secrets in their breasts, which they threatened to divulge.

In order that the full responsibility may be shown to rest upon the proper shoulders, the following extract is given from the Votes and Proceedings of the House of Commons of 3rd July, 1894. It is a motion of want of confidence, and all the Government supporters in the House voted against it :

" The Order of the day for the House to go again into Committee of Supply, being read :

" Sir John Thompson moved, That Mr. Speaker do now leave the Chair.

" Mr. Edgar moved in amendment thereto, that all the words " after the word "that" be left out, and the following inserted in- " stead thereof : "from the public trial and conviction of Thomas " McGreevy and N. K. Connolly for conspiracy to defraud, and " from evidence and papers already before this House, it appears " that large portions of the moneys which were found, upon said " trial, to have been criminally received by the said Thomas Mc-

" Greevy from Government contractors, were so received by him for
" the purpose of being expended in elections in the interest of the
" Conservative party, and for distribution by Sir Hector Langevin,
" M. P., and Sir Adolphe Caron, M.P., for the election of themselves
" and of other supporters of the Government at the general elec-
" tions held in February, 1887."

" That it further appears that large portions of the said
" moneys, together with other large sums collected by Sir Adolphe
" Caron from those interested in Government railway subsidies,
" were expended and distributed by Sir Hector Langevin and Sir
" Adolphe Caron, and in lavish and illegal amounts, to assist in
" the election of themselves and of other supporters of the Govern-
" ment, in the district of Quebec, at the general elections of 1887."

" That the said Sir Hector Langevin and Sir Adolphe Caron
" were then, and are now, members of this House, and on the roll of
" Her Majesty's Privy Councillors for Canada, and the said Sir
" Adolphe Caron is a Cabinet Minister and Postmaster General."

" That in the opinion of this House, the said Sir Hector Lan-
" gevin and Sir Adolphe Caron are deserving of the severest
" censure for their connection with the said transactions, and
" that it is a public scandal and an injury to the reputation of
" Canada that Sir Adolphe Caron should continue to hold the
" position of a Minister of the Crown."

"And the question being put on the amendment; in was
negatived on division."

### Bowell and the Blind Shares.

In 1882 a craze set in for the formation of Colonization Companies in the North-west.    The plan was to secure an Order-in-
Council from the Dominion Government granting large tracts of
land at low prices to individuals who would then form a joint
steck company to buy out their grants.    For this purpose a member of the House of Commons, now deceased, associated himself
with Mr. James C. Jamieson, a son-in-law of Sir Mackenzie
Bowell, then and now a Minister of the Crown, and they pro-
cured for themselves and ten others in April, 1882, an Order in
Council granting them several townships of very choice land. Mr.
Bowell was consulted about it before the Order in Council was
passed, and knew of the exceedingly advantageous "deal" that
had been arranged for the profit of his supporter in the House,
and for his son-in-law.   Both of those gentlemen were to receive
what was called "blind shares" in the stock of the company,

that is, stock on which they were to receive all the profits without paying any money into the company. A company called "The Prince Albert Colonization Company" was accordingly organized with twelve shareholders, ten of whom were paying parties, and the aforesaid two gentlemen were non-paying holders of "blind shares," each to the extent of $33,000.

It is true that Mr. Jamieson had to pay another party $500 to get in on the ground floor, but so warm an interest was taken by Mr. Bowell in this clever scheme of making money out of the Government grant that he offered to lend, and did lend, to Mr. Jamieson this $500, which was afterwards repaid to Mr. Bowell, when Mr. Jamieson sold out his blind shores for cash.

On the demand of Mr. Edgar, M. P., these charges were referred for investigation to the Committee of Privileges and Elections. They were proved to be literally true; yet by a majority composed entirely of Ministers themselves, Mr. Bowell was whitewashed by the Committee, and his conduct was declared to be beyond reproach. This report was laid before the House of Commons on 18th May, 1886, but although the House sat until 2nd June, the Government did not dare to move for its adoption. The position therefore is that Sir Mackenzie Bowell was accused in the House of conduct of which he himself said : "These statements affect not only my position as a Minister of the Crown but my reputation as a public man." These charges, so serious and disgraceful to a Minister and a public man, stand of record yet against him on the journals of the House of Commons. They have not been dealt with by the House. Are they wiped out by reason of his elevation to the Senate? He allowed the Session and the Parliament, in which the charges were made, to pass without a move, satisfied apparently with the whitewash of a packed committee, and a verdict cast by his own colleagues on that committee. Is this the stainless Premier, the pure and lofty statesman, who leads the Conservative party of Canada to-day?

No wonder that he moved the resolution to burke enquiry into the charges made against his colleague Sir Adolphe Caron in 1892. "A fellow feeling made him wondrous kind."

### Corrupt Sale of Public Offices---The Cochrane Case.

From 1888 to 1890 the patronage of the County of East Northumberland was in the hands of Edward Cochrane, Conservative M. P. The completion of the Murray Canal gave a number of positions as keepers of swing bridges across the canal to be awarded to political supporters by Mr. Cochrane.

There was at that time also a vacancy to be filled by him in the position of keeper of the Presque Isle Light House.

A committee of Mr. Cochrane's supporters was organized for the express purpose of corruptly trafficking in these office and with the full knowledge of Mr. Cochrane they did corruptly sell and dispose of such offices.

Hedley Simpson paid $200 for the Light House position, and each of the following persons paid from $125 to $200 apiece for the petty positions of keepers of swing bridges, namely: Wesley Goodrich, John D. Clouston, William Brown, Robert May and Thomas Fitzgerald.

When Mr. Cochrane, M. P., was informed that the price of the berths had been duly paid, he recommended to the Government the appointment of these men, and the appointments were promptly made.

The proceeds of these corrupt sales were applied to the political purposes of the Conservative party in the riding, and in part to pay off a promissory note on which Mr. Cochrane, M. P., was personally liable.

Mr. M. C. Cameron, M. P., brought these matters before the House, and this flagrant and miserable abuse of patronage, and this sale of public offices was proved before a select committee of the House of Commons in 1891.˙ A mild censure of the system of sale of public offices was passed, but the whitewash brush was applied, and the Government majority refused to condemn the conduct of the member who not only escaped censure, but has been treated by his party as a martyr, a hero, and a victim of Grit persecution ever since.

### Buying Up a Member of Parliament.—The Turcotte Case.

Mr. A. J. Turcotte, the present M. P. for Montmorenci Co., was elected on 11th March, 1892. He is now a very active personal ally and supporter of Sir Adolphe Caron. At the time of his election he was carrying on a grocery business in Quebec in partnership with Mr. Provost. The firm then had a contract with the Government in the name of Mr Provost, for the supply of the militia at the Citidel of Quebec with groceries and provisions, and up to the dissolution of the firm on 2nd February, 1893, they received from the Government cheques amounting to $4,112.85. This amount was all paid over by the firm to Mr. Turcotte for his private benefit.

After the dissolution of the firm, Mr. Turcotte continued in the grocery business and supplied the Militia Department with the goods. For these he received all the payment for his own benefit, although the cheques, as before, continued to be issued in Mr. Provost's name, and were endorsed by him over to Mr. Turcotte who cashed them.

It is of course grossly improper for a member to be sitting in the House drawing pay from contracts let to him by the Ministers. He is in fact sold to them, and does not represent the people, but is the slave of the Government.

The law condems this sort of thing very clearly, for section 10 of the Independence of Parliament Act, says:

"No person, directly or indirectly, alone or with any other, by himself or by the interposition of any trustee or third party, holding or enjoying, undertaking or executing any contract or agreement, expressed or implied, with or for the Government of Canada on behalf of the Crown, or with or for any of the officers of the Government of Canada, for which any public money of Canada is to be paid, shall be eligible as a member of the House of Commons, or shall sit or vote in the said House."

Yet in spite of the plain language of the statute, the Government majority in the House on 13th July, 1894, was called upon to whitewash Mr. Turcotte in the face of sworn evidence proving the above facts.

On that date Mr. Edgar, M. P., moved a resolution declaring that Mr. Turcotte had forfeited his seat.

Four Conservative members refused to swallow the scandalous whitewashing vote, but all the rest were whipped into line, voted down Mr. Edgar's motion, and had to justify by their votes the clearest breach of the Independence of Parliament that was ever proved before a committee.

Under that precedent, members can be safely bought up by public money, like sheep in a market, to support any Government that happens to be in power.

## Favoritism and Extravagance.

The Hon. John Haggart, Minister of Railways and Canals, represented his present constituency of Lanark in 1882, and used his influence with the Government to induce them to undertake the construction, at public expense, of a short canal of six miles in length (called the Tay canal) from the Rideau canal to the town of Perth, with a branch to Mr. Haggart's own mill in that town. The estimated cost inclusive of certain land and damages, was $132,660. The actual cost has amounted to the enormous sum of $476,128.

Is this immense expenditure justified by traffic upon the Tay canal ? On the contrary it is navigated only by some skiffs, one scow, two yachts and two tugs. The total revenue from this canal for the year ending Jan. 1st, 1894, was $135.76, while the actual cost of maintenance was for this same period, $2,486.00. Here is an instance of grossly excessive expenditure which lays the member who forced it upon the Government for his own advantage, open to the charge of being utterly unfit to manage the Department of Railways and Canals.

A resolution condemning that expenditure was moved in 1894 by Mr. John Charlton, M. P., but was voted down by the usual Government majority.

## Curran Bridge Scandal.

The story of the construction of two Government bridges over the Lachine canal (commonly called the Curran bridges), involves as startling a disclosure of incompetence, extravagance and criminal neglect of duty as has yet been made in Canada. The responsible head of the Department is Honorable John Haggart, Minister of Railways and Canals. and the work was all done in the city of Montreal, within telephoning distance of the Minister's office. The bridges were constructed during the first four months of the year 1893. The Department decided to have the work on the sub-structures of the bridges done by day labor. The contract was entered into with a contractor named St. Louis, a Government election pusher, who carried out the work as laid out by the Department and under its superintendence and direction.

The original estimate of cost of these sub-structures was $122,000, but the account presented to the Department for that work have amounted to $430,325, and of this sum $394,000 has actually been paid to the contractor by the Government.

In order to illustrate the nature of the outrageous overcharges a few examples may be given. The supply of timber and lumber paid for is over 1,000,000 feet, board measure, more than could have been used in those works. The cost of stone cutting on one of the bridges, if it had been let at the usual prices by piece work, would have been $3,000, whereas the amount paid by the Government, including the contractor's price is $16,715, and the cost of stone cutting on the other bridge was still more excessive. The prices paid by the Department to the contractor for labor were greatly beyond current prices, in some instances being as high as $12 for work for which the contractor only paid $4.50, and $9.20 for other work for which the contractor only paid $3.75. False pay lists were made up with the names of hundreds and thousands of men upon them who never worked at all, and very many of whom were entirely fictitious.

No check was kept by any Government official upon these lists, or upon the number of men employed. For months the contractor, St. Louis, was allowed to charge just what number of men he liked, and these pay sheets were duly certified by the Government officials as correct, and paid by the Government. One official swore that he kept a private memorandum of the numbers of men employed each day for some weeks. On comparing this the truth of which was sworn to, with the Government returns, it was found that where 10 men were actually employed 30 were charged for, and where 30 were actually employed 90 or 100 were charged, and where 100 were employed 300 or 400 were charged.

It was the most open, bare-faced swindle ever exposed in Canada, and to this day not one of the culprits has been convicted in court or punished. A pretence has been made of beginning a prosecution against St. Louis, but it is only a pretence. The elections will soon be over, and if the Government is sustained, Mr. Ouimet will take good care that his cousin St. Louis, does not suffer. The Government Commissioners, Messrs. McLeod, Douglas and Veniot, appointed to examine into the facts, reported that the amount stolen was $195,693.

This was a larger sum than the whole work could have been completed for had it been built by contract in the usual way.

These facts cannot be contradicted or denied, as they have been proved on several occasions, and Mr. Haggart, while not denying them, is pursuing a somewhat cowardly course of throwing the whole blame upon subordinate officers of his Department.

The people of Canada, however, pay Mr. Haggart a very large salary for looking after this business for them, and it is a monstrous proposition that he, the responsible Minister of the Crown, should be able to clear his skirts by blaming subordinate officers and contractors whom he appointed and paid. Mr. St. Louis, the contractor, excuses himself on the ground that he was forced to contribute so much money to the election of the Conservative party that he had to make it up out of contracts. In order to avoid the exposure of particulars of his political contributions all his books connected with the matter were burnt. It is possible that the inward history of this disgraceful transaction will never be known, but the Government and their followers who defended it by their votes last session, will be held to strict account when they appear before their electors. Sir Richard Cartwright, on the 18th July, 1894, moved a resolution in the House of Commons exposing and condemning this transaction, but it was voted down by the usual Government majority.

## Refusal of Enquiry.

When charges of misconduct have been made against Ministers in the House of Commons, the Government have sometimes altered the charges. There is another instance where a serious charge was made against a Minister of the Crown, and the Government called on their majority in Parliament to vote down and refuse any inquiry whatever into the matters charged. This was notably the case when in 1891 Mr. J. F. Lister, M.P., brought serious charges against Hon. John Haggart in connection with the Section B. contract. On the 13th September, 1891, he made the following motion :

"That James Frederick Lister, Esquire, the member representing the electoral district of West Lambton in this House, having declared from the seat in this House that he is credibly informed, and that he believes that he is able to establish by satisfactory evidence :

"That in the year 1879 Messrs. Alexander Manning, Alexander Shields, John James Macdonald, Alexander McDonell, James Isbester and Peter McLaren entered into a contract with the Government of Canada for the construction of a portion of the Canadian Pacific Railway between Port Arthur and Rat Portage, known as Section B.

"The said contract and the works in connection therewith were completed by the said contractors to whom they were a source of great profit.

"During the whole period covered by the said contract, the Honorable John G Haggart, now Postmaster-General and a member of Her Majesty's Privy Council for Canada, was a member of the House of Commons for the South Riding of Lanark, and still is such member.

"That the said Honorable John G. Haggart became and was beneficially interested in the profits of said contract which accrued to the share thereof standing in the name of the said Peter McLaren, and has received large sums out of the said profits, and has otherwise derived direct and substantial pecuniary benefits therefrom

"That during the progress of the said works, and while the said Honorable John G. Haggart was so interested therein, members of the said firm were called upon by members of the Government of Canada for large contributions for political purposes, and such contributions were paid out of the moneys of the said firm, and with the knowledge and assent of the said Honorable John G. Haggart were charged against the profits of the firm; and while the said contributions were so demanded and paid, the said firm of contractors were in various ways dependent upon the Government by reason of many matters being unsettled and in dispute in relation to the said contract, which were at the time of such contributions or subsequently settled not unfavorably to the said contractors

"That a Select Committee be appointed to enquire fully into the said allegations, with the power to send for persons, papers and records, and to examine witnesses upon oath or affirmation, and to employ shorthand writers to take down such evidence as they may deem necessary, and to have the evidence printed from day to day for the use of the Committee, and that the Committee do report in full the evidence taken before them, and all their proceedings on the reference, and the result of their enquiries, and that rule 78 of this House

as to the selection of committees be suspended and that the said committee be composed of Messrs. Mills (Bothwell), Edgar, Barron, Lister (who shall not have the right to vote), Dickey, Wood (Brockville), Girouard and McLeod."
This motion was voted down by the usual Government majority.

## Public Expenditure Has Increased Alarmingly.

Since Confederation in 1867, the public expenditure has increased alarmingly. Commencing with $13,486,092 in 1867-8, it had risen to $37,585,025 in 1893-4. On July 1st. 1868, the estimated population of the Dominion was 3,520,000. On July 1st, 1894, the estimated population was but little over 5,000,000, showing an increase of population during the period a fraction over 42 per cent, while the increase of expenditure for the same period was $24,098,933, or 178 per cent. The increase of the net debt during the same period was $170,454,588, or 225 per cent.

Mr. Mackenzie came into office November 8th, 1873. The expenditure for that fiscal year amounted to $23,316,316, 1877-8 was his last full fiscal year in office and the expenditure for that year was $23,503,158. An increase for the term of only $186,842. For a portion of the fiscal year ending June 30th, 1878, Mr. Mackenzie's administration was responsible as it held office till October 10th, 1878, making three months and ten days of the year, and if a comparatively exact statement of the increase of expenditure under Mr. Mackenzie's administration is desired, the supply bill for 1878 9 will furnish the data.

In no year during Mr. Mackenzie's administration did the expenditure exceed the amount of the supply bill for that year. The supply bill for 1878-9 amounted to $23,669,000, and his administration would not have exceeded that amount Had he remained in office therefore till July 1st, 1879, the increase of expenditure during his administration would have been $353,000. That the expenditure for 1878-9 actually reached the sum of $24,455,381 is due to the fact that for nine months of year Mr. Mackenzie's successors administered the finances.

During Mr. Mackenzie's administration the contracts and obligations left by his predecessors rendered an increase of the debt necessary, and of course rendered an addition to the annual interest charge unavoidable, but so great was the economy and prudence of his administration that during his term of office, the controllable expenditure was reduced by the sum of $1,781,000, and the taxation from cus toms duties fell from $14,325,192 in 1873-4 to $12,900,659 in 1878-9, a decrease of $1,424,533.

By selecting the period commencing July 1st, 1881, and ending July 1st, 1891, an exact comparison can be made for the decande between the increase of debt, of expenditure, and of customs taxation on the one hand and the increase of population on the other hand.

| | | | |
|---|---|---|---|
| Population, 1881, | - | - | 4,324,810 |
| Population, 1891, | - | - | 4,832,236 |
| Increase, | - | - | 508,429 |
| Percentage of increase, | | - | 11·66 |

```
Net debt, 1881,          -        -        $155,395,780
    "      1891,          -        -         237,809,030
        Increase,             -        $82,413,250
        Percentage of increase,       53
Expenditure, 1881,        -        -        $25,502,554
    "        1891,        -        -         36,343,567
        Increase of expenditure,      $10,841,013
        Percentage of increase,       42
Taxation by customs duties, 1881,           $18,406,092
    "        "         "    1891,            23,399,300
        Increase,             -        $4,993,208
        Percentage of increase,       27
```

### Increase of the Controllable Expenditure.

The statistics relating to the increase of the controllable expenditure since 1878 are of a most unsatisfactory character. The increase of population between July 1st, 1878, and July 1st, 1893, have not exceeded 21 per cent. advance upon the population in the first year named. During the same period the proportion of increase in controllable expenditure has been very much greater. In 1878 the expenditure on account of Administration of Justice, Arts, Agriculture and Statistics, Fisheries, Quarantine, Indians, Legislation, Militia and Defence, Public Works, Superannuation, Excise, N rthwest Territories Government, Mail subsidies and Steamship subventions, Civil Government, Adulteration of Food, Mounted Police and Miscellaneous amounted to $5,256,424. The expenditure for the same purposes in 1893 amounted to $10,384,272, an increase of 97 per cent. during a period when the population increased 21 per cent. Some of the items of increase need no comment as will be seen by reference to the following statement:

```
Arts, Agriculture and Statistics, 1878............$ 92,365
  "        "            "      1893............ 258,635
        Increase...................$166,270
        Percentage of increase.......180
Fisheries, 1878.............................$ 93,262
    "      1893............................ 482,381
        Increase....................$389,119
        Percentage of increase........417
Quarantine, 1878............................$ 26,340
    "       1893............................ 101,954
        Increase....................$ 76,610
        Percentage of increase........287
Indians, 1878..............................$421,503
    "    1893.............................. 956,552
        Increase....................$535,049
        Percentage of increase........126
```

Militia and Defence, 1878...................................................$ 618,136
    "       "       1893.............................................1,419,745
      Increase................................$801,609 .
      Percentage of increase.............129
Public Works, 1878...........................................................$997,469
    "     "    1893..........................................1,927,832 .
      Increase.................................$930,363
      Percentage of increase..............93
Superannuation, 1878.......................................................$106,588
    "        1893............................................... 263,710
      Increase................................$157,122
      Percentage of increase................147
Excise, 1878....................................................................$215,024
    "   1893 ........................................... 387,673
      Increase...............................$179,649
      Percentage of increase...............80
Northwest Territories Government, 1878............. $ 18,199
    "      "      "   1893................ 276,446
      Increase.............................$258,247 ,
      Percentage of increase...........1,420
Civil Government, 1878.........................................$ 823.369
    "     "    1893............................1,367,570
      Increase.............................$544,201
      Percentage of increase...............66
Mounted Police, 1878....................................$334,748
    "     "   1893................................. 615,479
      Increase..............................$280,748
      Percentage of increase...............83

It is time to call a halt. The march of corruption has been continued too long. With increase in debt, expenditure and taxation, so far outstripping increase of population, the result, if we do not change our course, will be serious if not disastrous. Already the consequences of extravagance and currupt waste of money and resources are severely felt. The population of the country is at a standstill. Without increase of population our undeveloped resources cannot be utilized. Without a radical reform in the administration of our public affairs the increase of population and the corresponding increase of wealth and property will be meagre and insatisfactory. Is it not time for patriotic citizens of all shades of politics to give the situation of the country careful consideration, and is it not evident that the record made by the party in power since 1878, warrants the belief that the principles, the purposes, and the methods of its leaders now in office render them incapable of giving the country an honest and economical administration of its affairs? To other men must be assigned the task of extricating the country from the difficulties that now confront it.

# INDEX.